Beyond Capitalism

Giulio Sapelli

Beyond Capitalism

Machines, Work and Property

palgrave
macmillan

Giulio Sapelli
University of Milan
Milano, Italy

Translation by Juliet Haydock
Editing by Barbara Racah

ISBN 978-3-030-20768-7 ISBN 978-3-030-20769-4 (eBook)
https://doi.org/10.1007/978-3-030-20769-4

This Palgrave Macmillan imprint is published by the registered company Springer Nature Switzerland AG.
The registered company address is: Gewerbestrasse 11, 6330 Cham, Switzerland

For Bruno Amoroso
In memoriam

Preface

Markets, politics, crisis

The debate on globalisation and financial capitalism rages on, producing unsound scientific results and fuelling popular beliefs.

This book puts things on a much sounder footing by adopting a meticulously interdisciplinary approach and rejecting the one-track way of thinking that has dominated the world for the past 30 years, cutting us off from what we know about society and its economic relations.

The one-track approach essentially espouses an individualist and behaviourist approach to analysis and methodology and anthropomorphises everything from a materialist and consumerist viewpoint (limitless individual rationalisation for maximising financial utility).

My way of thinking is based on the belief that the economy is only part of society: it is determined by society and therefore by interpersonal relationships and personal behaviour. I am entirely against tired old Marxist hypotheses, as well as neoclassical ideas inspired by neo-liberal ideology. According to popular belief, globalisation is a predominantly new, predominantly economic phenomenon that emerged from the relentless race towards modernity, went one step further (post-modernity) and morphed into contemporary capitalism.

My thinking eschews popular belief and aims to lay the foundations for a scientific exploration that goes beyond preconceptions and dumbing-down.

This work overturns many clichés of popular belief and turns the world off its head, on which many would have it standing, and places it upon its feet—to dust off a metaphor used by a long-forgotten classic of philosophy (Feuerbach, Ludwig Andreas, Zur Kritik der Hegelschen Philosophie [Towards a Critique of Hegel's Philosophy] in Arnold Ruge's Jahrbücher, Zurich, 1839).

The world seems upside down to us partly because written histories are no longer part of the toolkit of knowledge considered essential by those in charge at every level of organisation.

Knowledge is never a linear, narrow, cold process.

Knowledge, even if we are unaware of it, is always a hot-blooded, dense, snagged and tortuous process that shapes cultures (in the full anthropological sense of the word) rather than skills and capacities.

Overlooking written histories and living and working with a disregard for history deprive the act of being in the world of its deeper meaning. It is like finding oneself in the middle of a series of paintings without any perspective, like Byzantine icons frozen by divine grace. Yet when the paintings paraded before us are not saints and icons of the Orthodox calendar but the turbulent vicissitudes of life, this pre-Renaissance lack of perspective can have devastating consequences for those in a position to steer events. Such people hail their successes but are really ruled by chance. They claim victory by distorting events to create an illusory narrative that has nothing to do with the reality. The resulting communication processes warp minds and peddle fairy tales instead of truthful narratives. So it is with globalisation.

We need to add some perspective to the picture: history did not end with the collapse of the USSR, and globalisation is simply a cyclical recurrence of events that great contemporary historians have already documented in extraordinary works that should not be left to gather dust.

Past periods of booming commercial trade, unfettered by barriers and tariffs, were the great drivers of economic growth and cultural mingling.

This melting pot could not have come about without the trade routes—Montesquieu's "douce commerce"—which looked all set to achieve the Masonic dream, infinite as history itself, of overcoming national boundaries.

Modern capitalism arose between the second half of the nineteenth century and World War I, underpinned by the myth and reality of free trade and British world domination, then fell to pieces following the post-war collapse of the empires with shattering consequences that lasted until the 1940s.

The fact that the machinery of globalisation (affecting industry and services as well as finance) was set in motion after the end of the 1980s merely proves that globalisation is a phenomenon with roots that are more political and cultural than economic. Without the collapse of the Soviet Union, the uncertain path of European unity, so asymmetrical and strongly governed by the presence of nation states, would not have even got off the ground; things would have stopped with the Common Market.

However, the weakening world trade cycle meant the Masonic dream was stillborn, killed off by the dazzle of monetarist functionalism. Most importantly, without the decline and fall of the USSR, world trade would not have got back on its feet and achieved growth close to that of the boom years of the nineteenth and early twentieth centuries. This came about despite deep crises and setbacks and continued undeterred even in the face of the Franco-German, Russian and Italian armies and the irretrievable break and deep schism that occurred as Communism spawned a series of increasingly warmongering states. The Communism in question was more Asian than European, more Russian than internationalist. It became stripped of its utopian connotations and soon turned into dictatorial dominion by force to an extent hitherto unseen in the history of industrial societies. Only China faces a higher stage of terrorist domination, mixed with mass grassroots acceptance by hundreds of millions of human beings.

Globalisation as a political phenomenon, and thus as a specific historical phenomenon, cannot be reduced to graphs that measure effects but tell us nothing about causes or, to return to our metaphor, transmute the epistemological process into a series of icons instead of an array of paintings executed with Renaissance perspective.

This book remains true to the classical economic approach.

Firstly, it portrays the economy as what it really is and not what those who hold the most potent means of training minds (the great world universities) and communication (mass media for the masses) would have us believe: a reality and a series of theories that are cut off from the moral, because they are cut off from the human element and devoid of the personal.

The economy is simply the incarnation of a moral philosophy based on an anthropological image of mankind. This is true even if those who are supposed to be in the know, in today's increasingly self-referential and fragmented world of social differentiation, are unaware of it, given the breathtaking ignorance of the many.

Neoclassical and neo-liberal economists see the individual as a formulaic liberal archetype. Classical economists and philosophers of being believe that individuals cannot be reduced to formulas or cloned.

Christian personalism or humanism is, by definition, based on the person.

So it follows that the economy is, by definition, an economy that is not for profit but for people—in theory and in practice. In theory, the market can only be a probabilistic event, always tending towards perfection, often dominated by rampant imperfection and above all subject to the cyclical nature of growth as well as of depression and crisis.

This theoretical approach fits the Zeitgeist rising from the ruins of the great crisis: firstly because of the people's resistance to the crisis (they are revealing very strong and often unexpected resilience, associating and joining forces more than is apparent at first glance); secondly because of the transformation clearly reflected by the real economy network made up of finance, manufacturing and services—and thirdly because of the cultures emerging from the crisis: cooperative, giving cultures that are not even theoretically possible according to a mainstream neoclassical view—and when they do exist are invisible.

Globalisation[1] itself is changing under the effects of the great ongoing global crisis. This is happening because we are seeing the end of a *political* cycle: not merely that of the long *economic* cycle that befuddled minds and paralysed would-be virtuous behaviour because of the overriding compulsion to repeat the cycle of private borrowing and risk.

The key to this long economic and political cycle was the conviction—bolstering capitalist thinking in the UK, the US and Germany—that world growth could only be achieved by fighting inflation and particularly public debt.

Instead, growth flagged: income moved from labour to capital, weakening the demand creditworthiness of markets while finance drained resources from industry, generating employment stagnation that state-of-the-art services could not entirely compensate for.

The long economic and political cycle floundered. Its new centre was the international market, which could no longer operate as a regulatory mechanism for state powers and internal growth mechanisms, let alone trade.

European market unification through the Treaty of Maastricht in 1992 represented the culmination of this international policy. Unsurprisingly, those were the years of rampant stock market growth and the "New Economy". Europe became a very sensitive link in this new economic and political perspective.

At its centre lay electoral consensus ruled by the markets. The present cycle has now lasted 30 years.

The political face of that cycle began at the beginning of the 1990s, when the great institutional investors, the great business bankers of the English-speaking world and the great West European democracies, led by France and Germany, imposed a single currency in Europe and a social discipline based on the rigour of public accounting.

All these rulers and builders of the globalising markets were responsible for introducing what amounted to liberalist totalitarianism.

In other words, a totalitarian means of establishing a market in a democracy.

This description might sound like an oxymoron but actually reflects the polyarchic and undemocratic face of global capitalist order: a single thought, single market rule in a democratic procedural order conditioned by de facto situational powers that are public, not private. The European oligarchic functional autonomies are also public. They masquerade as technocracies but are actually a mixture of second-degree democratic representation based on party politics and regulatory powers co-opted without democratic legitimacy.

The prevailing order is continually conditioned by de facto situational powers that remain hidden from view while regulating the travesties that masquerade as procedures.

This method of imposed market lies at the root of the decadence in which we are currently floundering.

A society caught in such a vice can no longer produce anything meaningful thus lacks vital motivation: meaning has become separated from function.

The market governed itself, picking off the weakest and allowing victory to the ruling polyarchies. Profit became a vortex, an illusory ability to rule risk. It became a weapon of mass destruction: blindness in the face of spreading relative poverty that could not be exorcised by reducing absolute poverty. It became an obstacle to any transformation that could avert imminent collapse.

The options presented to the world at the beginning of the noughties were to change or fall into the abyss. There was no way out.

The failing technocracy taught in our business schools collapsed. The plebiscitary democracy that was supposed to become the most relevant political mechanism for the emergence of a society of rights also collapsed. This type of society is now commensurate with a full-blown market that can only be based on infringing the purchasing rights of billions of consumers.

When confidence in uninterrupted consumption collapses, plebiscitary democracy remains and Tocqueville's "conditions of equality" stand revealed as an insidious instrument of standardisation unless they are sustained by a strong, stable state of law.

Even this has been destroyed by the rampant market: the only rights left are those of traders. This is not enough to govern society.

After a series of events, new political forces found their feet throughout the world and had to carry out the work of government driven by moral suasion from the great international market rulers.

Hence the divergence between the two-headed dog of state: representation becomes entangled in reducible complexity, only allowing decisions for their own sake (Schmitt's Utopia according to Luhmann[2]). And when the decision is made, it absorbs and fades the fabric of participation… This clearly shows that making money rather than labour central to social organisation has had devastating consequences. Money cannot reclassify social castes, roles and functions, because it is not able to regroup the social and give it a reproducible community meaning.

Nomadism and the apparently unstoppable perpetuation of inequality that becomes the essence of ruling social positions have had disastrous effects that are still submerging us, in a world where only faith can save us.

At the beginning of the disastrous 30-year period, politics began to go silent when and where it was needed most.

It had been exercising its power, but that power has been ephemeral, propagating only self-referential political classes (this is why Luhmann's teachings on autopoiesis are still relevant).

So now the voice of the market is the only one we hear.

The privatisations began against this backdrop of political aphasia and unbridled market-oriented discourse, which had to be implemented through the allocation of ownership rights.

The liberalisations actually began amidst unprecedented difficulties that increased as market power was depleted, but they were always heralded as saving the day.

The power of the new Caesarist democracy did the rest: a myth grew of a kind of sovereignty that has legitimacy not in the general interest but in the interests of a special club, of people hungry for favours, of an economic society, not a society civilised by a passive, unspoken belief in legality.

The sovereignty of business and trade thus began to be no longer market based, as was the case at the beginning of the first cycle mentioned above. It was no longer based on a daily effort to make those markets less imperfect but on the principle of immediate decision-making, no longer bound by representation except when attributing the principle of legitimacy that the state is bound to hold with the advent of mass societies.

This intersection gradually began to legitimatise the market as a mechanism for regulating macroeconomic decisions over tax and expenditure.

Recent world events stemming from the need to support consumer society, the aggressive, lemming-like society of unlimited rights and, above all, financial circulation under the uncontrolled rule of major global bankers must be interpreted as part of this general transformation.

This does not affect only Europe and the US, but the whole world, led by BRICS and then ASEAN. This is even truer since the recent EU enlargement, which nipped the possible future of European markets in the bud.

The European constitution is emblematic of this cycle of separating politics from economy, now coming to an end.

A global solution to the crisis legitimised by the principle of representation was late in coming in the wake of financial scandals essentially caused by a lack of internal controls by companies.

This paralysis served to discredit the political class we see chattering all over our newspapers and TVs and also, paradoxically, the state authorities that are attacked and vilified without being able to come up with any quick and revitalising decisions.

The unsurprising outcome of all this is global growth in judicial power. This increasingly corporate power tramples on Montesquieu's theory of the separation of powers every day while unscrupulously invoking him and setting out to govern or offer to the highest bidder a neo-barbarian judicial stamp of approval in the name of the common people.

When short-circuited by politics, market sovereignty thus loses any semblance of legitimacy. Every day it is discredited and corrupted. All this is part of a transformation of the system of weights and balances intrinsic to the global geo-strategic situation that is happening at an unprecedented rate.

This book proposes a way out of the crisis that can briefly be described as reviving a form of modern community-based, non-State socialism that is antithetical to Lassallism (the strategy of pursuing socialism through the use of the state). This is very different from the form of socialism with an impeccable intellectual pedigree that is being brought back into vogue by the bold upholders of great Labour thinking in the wake of Blair's barbarism, namely the revival of an economy that can be planned and regulated by state-of-the-art hi-tech tools.[3]

This prospect is more interesting and respectable than ever. It assumes that the contradiction between the boom in productive forces—meaning artificial intelligence and big data—and the increasing social inefficiency of capitalist property allocation (with structural mass unemployment and an increase in relative poverty) will increasingly lead to radical systemic unsustainability.

A reformed capitalist approach is impossible according to this viewpoint, though I will argue otherwise in this book. I believe that reforming, not governing, through political struggle and creating economic segments alternative to the dominant approach is still possible.

The alternative, for supporters of these ideas,[4] is a fast-track, Communist alternative, implementing forms of self-government, certainly, but in a context of a planned economy made possible now and in the future through steady progress in telecommunications technologies, artificial intelligence and computer science. These are enablers of "economic calculation in the socialist commonwealth". The Soviet collapse was an outcome of the global civil war between communism and capitalism that saw the end of the socialist attempt, worn down by military competition and lack of the technological basis necessary to enable the economic calculation. The debate on economic calculation in the socialist commonwealth taken up at the beginning of the twentieth century and then in the 1930s, firstly by Enrico Barone[5] Enrico Barone and then by the Austrian School was resumed with intellectual vigour. The development of productive forces now makes a planned economy possible.

The economic calculation thesis cannot be fudged: the development of productive forces would make the sums add up, which would enable us to do without the capitalist form of allocating ownership rights to varying extents depending on political choices.

However, if this were to come about, the historical opposition between Trotskyism and Bordighism, on the one hand, and Stalinism on the other hand, would reopen. This would be inevitable because the bureaucracy or technocracy that would govern this technological power would be mortally opposed to the very idea of representative democracy, although the fate that now awaits United Europe, as a technical construct without democratic political legitimacy, is an equally well-documented fact. Europe is now a non-democratic polyarchy. The same would happen with this form of communism: humanity would simply find itself faced with a new form of slavery that would be far worse than capitalist slavery. It would fatally endanger the very idea of socialism, whatever the economic basis for the resulting socioeconomic construct. The danger of declining into an administered rather than a planned economy would be enormous and democracy, which is commensurate with socialism and constitutes its beating heart, would be in grave peril.

The prospect of potentially segmenting economic planning should be implemented only in the context of community-based socialism based on non-capitalist forms of allocating property rights that are managed democratically and not technocratically.

This could support and help determine significant segments of the new economic policy that must be established if we are not to sink into barbarism.

When discussing the prospects of capitalism, the topic of global and European recovery crops up on a regular basis.

This is always statistically accurate but incorrect from a general historical and economic viewpoint.

The recovery is and will be forced into the vortex of world deflation generated by the neoclassical, overriding counterrevolution of financial capitalism, on the one hand, and German-influenced European ordoliberalism on the other.

All this plunges the world into lower salaries and a global contraction of fixed capital or what Marx and Ricardo termed "dead labour".

This recovery would mean yet another colossal shift of wealth from labour to capital, on a global scale.

All this is taking place in a world that, fortunately for us, is growing demographically despite the falling European population, but which must therefore always find new resources for hope to spring eternal.

This book advocates a form of neo-socialism with a market increasingly counterbalanced by growth, certain of a new role for the entrepreneurial state,[6] but implemented by creating new ways of allocating property rights with a revival of intermediate bodies and workers' organisations, irrespective of the degree to which workers are included in the mechanism of capitalist accumulation.

This is the inspiration for Chap. 6 of this book entitled:

Blowing into the bottle. Olivetti rediscovered, or the syntax of hope. (Adriano Olivetti: temptation of betrayal).

This is a mark of intellectual loyalty to a political and moral legacy that has profoundly influenced my whole life.

It has been a long and impervious path, but I feel compelled to forge ahead, despite the reactionary broadsides aimed on a daily basis against those who refuse to bow to the state of regression imposed by the current refusal to think outside the box.

University of Milan
Milano, Italy

Giulio Sapelli

Bibliography

M. Mann, The Sources of Social Power, vol. 4: Globalization, 1945–2011, Cambridge University Press, Cambridge–New York, 2013.

N. Luhmann, *Vertrauen – ein Mechanismus der Reduktion sozialer Komplexität.* Enke, Stuttgart, 1968.

P. Cockshott, A. Cottrell, H. Dieterich, *Transition to 21st Century Socialism in the European Union*, Amazon Fullfiment, Wroclaw, 2010. For a view more in line with my own, see P. Mason, *Postcapitalism. A Guide to Our Future,* Allen, London, 2015.

P. Cockshott and M. Nieto, *Ciber-comunismo. Planificacion economica, computadoras y democracia*, Editorial Trotta, Madrid, 2017.

E. Barone, *Il ministro della produzione nello stato collettivista*, in "Giornale degli economisti", s. II, 1908, pp. 267–93, 391–414 (revisited in E.Barone., *Le opere economiche*, edited by A. Piperno, 1st vol., *Scritti vari*, Zanichelli, Bologna 1936, pp. 231–97.

M. Mazzuccato, *The Entrepreneurial State*, Demos, London, 2011.

Contents

Introduction to the Book by Giulio Sapelli

For Bruno Amoroso. It could not be otherwise. Giulio Sapelli was bound to dedicate his brilliant, passionate and well-researched reflection on our contemporary age to Bruno Amoroso, eminent Danish/Italian economist, expert on globalisation and self-styled "Intruder" (from the title of his memoirs "Memoirs of an Intruder"). The complexity of Sapelli's book is clear from the title. Can we say that capitalism is over? And what was it really all about? These smaller questions are merely appetisers for the big, earth-shaking question of what will come after, or what there is "beyond capitalism"? To come up with answers, we must have a clear idea of what capitalism is today and what it was in the twentieth century. And no one is better equipped to tell us than Giulio Sapelli.

Quoting Pope Benedict XVI's *Caritas in veritate* encyclical, Sapelli wrote that Bruno Amoroso's most important intellectual and moral legacy was his belief that "only the truth sets us free". Reading the world truthfully in order to find freedom is the compass that guides Sapelli through his analytical journey. I am not exaggerating when I say the final result is as lucid as it is powerful. He has gazed beyond the confines of the single-track thinking that has made human reasoning lazy and impoverished to the point of aridity over the last 30 years. The same does not apply to Sapelli's reasoning, which remains as alert and critical as ever, as is clear from reading this book.

If his evangelical and moral quest for the truth, strenuously avoiding common sense clichés, is his compass, the primary goal of his proposed journey is to demonstrate that the economy is part of society but not all of it. It is partly determined by relationships, behaviour and the multiple variables that make up a reality that is not simple, nor can it be simplified: the author states in his foreword what should be evident to everyone, "knowledge is never a linear, narrow, cold process". This *should* be evident, but this is far from the truth. In 2017, the Noble Prize for economics was at last awarded to someone who took a closer look at the subject and confounded popular belief by concluding that economic and financial choices are not automatically rational but can only be explained by inter-relating economics, psychology, mathematics and humanity. Thanks to Richard Thaler and everyone who voted to award him the Nobel Prize, people are starting to question the dogma on free-market efficiency whereby mathematical and rational patterns can be applied to maximise profit, which will in turn maximise well-being for everyone.

Back in 2009, another Nobel laureate, Elinor Ostrom, argued free riders do not always look after their own personal interests rather than those of the community. Ostrom was ahead of her time in arguing that unselfish forms of behaviour in the interests of general well-being are possible. She maintained that reality is much too varied and broad to be described and encapsulated by theory. Objective experience shows numerous successful instances of collective resource management in different social and cultural settings at different latitudes. Back in 2009, Ostrom believed it was unthinkable to have a single benchmark economic model. She believed that it is possible and even desirable for many different forms to coexist, each representing optimum institutional solutions to the numerous and various problems of society. The crisis has made our society even more fragile and defenceless, and this is precisely why we need to move away from past dogmas to find new and different responses.

Sapelli thoroughly dismantles the line of thought based on the supposed logical and mathematical consequentiality of history, which considers globalisation to be a purely economic and new phenomenon that emerged in modern times due to the fall of the USSR. Even though this is not true, the error of interpretation (a mistake made by individuals and a product of the one-track thinking that has done so much damage) is again the upshot of considering economics to be a mathematical model divorced from human beings and humankind and as such unfettered by any principles of accountability. This ingrained model can only result in neo-mercantile financial capitalism, which sees the spread of digital technology as a "growing fantasy" ruling expectations of an equally gloomy future instead of an instrument of liberation. Such mathematical models cannot explain how it is imaginable for us to have a society in which 0.1% of the population owns the machines, 0.9% manage them and the remaining 99% "will languish in the abyss of unemployment". Sapelli is unafraid to speak of the "tartar steppes"[7] that will arise as a natural and devastating consequence of the "smart machinery revolution".

Sapelli's almost fleeting reference to Theodore Adorno, citing his work *Minima Moralia*, is neither random nor incidental. Adorno dedicated this work to his friend and collaborator Max Horkheimer, as if hinting to his readers that they should explore an analysis that prophetically foresaw the developments of the short twentieth century and the emerging drifts of the next one. With its prescient subtitle "Reflections on a damaged life", the German philosopher in exile in the US during World War II got to the heart of the matter and Sapelli, as the eclectic academic he is, deconstructs his work with reference to prominent passages. To echo Adorno, today "an honest life is no longer possible because we live in an inhuman society" and in the words of one of his most famous aphorisms, "the splinter in your eye is the best magnifying glass"; like the splinters of a mirror, Sapelli's book reflects the way of thinking that has emerged in recent decades, underpinned by a loss of the sense of giving that Adorno described so clearly: Human beings are forgetting how to give gifts. Violations of the exchange-principle have something mad and unbelievable about them; here and there even children size up the gift-giver mistrustfully, as if the gift were only a trick, to sell them a brush or soap (…). Real gift-giving had its happiness in imagining the happiness of the receiver. It meant choosing, spending time, going out of one's way, thinking of the other as a subject: the opposite of forgetfulness. Hardly anyone is still capable of this.

This bitter reflection dates back to the 1940s. The slow and inexorable progress of this inability that Sapelli describes in the book and unpicks for all to see was already evident among the most acute thinkers. With his trademark lightness of touch, Sapelli maintains hope intact. His fond view of hope harks back to one of France's best-loved poets Charles Péguy, who grew up in the school of Henry Bergson and fell on the first day of the dramatic battle of the Marne. Three years before that day, Péguy wrote in "The Portico of the Mystery of the Second Virtue": "What surprises me, says God, is hope.

And I can't get over it.

This little hope who seems like nothing.

This little girl hope.

Immortal". This hope is what Sapelli invites us to keep hold of, particularly when seeking to navigate the troubled waters of our times without capsizing.

by Giuseppe De Lucia Lumeno

Notes

1. One essential work of reference is M. Mann, The Sources of Social Power, vol. 4: Globalization, 1945–2011, Cambridge University Press, Cambridge–New York, 2013.
2. N. Luhmann, *Vertrauen – ein Mechanismus der Reduktion sozialer Komplexität*. Enke, Stuttgart, 1968.
3. P. Cockshott, A. Cottrell, H. Dieterich, *Transition to Twenty-first Century Socialism in the European Union*, Amazon Fullfiment, Wroclaw, 2010. For a view more in line with my own, see P. Mason, *Postcapitalism. A Guide to Our Future,* Allen, London, 2015.
4. The most eloquent and comprehensive work is by P. Cockshott and M. Nieto, *Ciber-comunismo. Planificacion economica, computadoras y democracia*, Editorial Trotta, Madrid, 2017.

5. E. Barone, *Il ministro della produzione nello stato collettivista*, in "Giornale degli economisti", s. II, 1908, pp. 267–93, 391–414 (revisited in E. Barone., *Le opere economiche*, edited by A. Piperno, 1st vol., *Scritti vari*, Zanichelli, Bologna, 1936, pp. 231–97.
6. M. Mazzuccato, *The Entrepreneurial State*, Demos, London, 2011.
7. The author refers to the Italian novel "Il deserto dei tartari" (The Tartar Steppes) by Dino Buzzati. This tells the story of a young officer, Giovanni Drogo, who is sent to a remote outpost overlooking a desolate Tartar desert. He spends his career waiting for the barbarian horde rumoured to live beyond the desert. When the attack by the Tartars finally arrives, Drogo falls ill and the new chieftain of the fortress dismisses him.

1

The Global Crisis Caused by Deflation

Transformation of Global Capitalism, Deflation with Unemployment and Rhetoric Around Intergenerational Conflict

A deep-seated global transformation has come about in the composition of capital: in percentage terms, capital expenditure for setting up mighty large-scale manufacturing industries has increasingly given way to a different type of capital expenditure to build a new service industry with lower fixed capital intensity and lower transaction costs.

This primarily came about due to the advent of the last of Kondratieff's[1] hypothesised wave cycles based on Information Communication Technology (ICT): a different organic capital composition led to a 30-year fall in global interest rates. This greatly benefited the high-risk financial component of modern capitalism, as we saw with the crisis caused by excess risk-taking that hit the globalised world after the deregulations of Clinton and Blair. This deregulation made it possible to mitigate the cyclical overproduction crisis due to low international

G. Sapelli, *Beyond Capitalism*, https://doi.org/10.1007/978-3-030-20769-4_1

consumption rates but nevertheless struck the globalised world like a hammer blow.

The financial sector cushioned the immediate effects of the crisis caused by failure to achieve a profit by securitising debts and delaying the fall of corporations, which promptly responded by expanding their financial returns, along with their industrial returns.

On the other hand, the monetary expansion policy advocated by the Federal Reserve persuaded international capitalists not to remove capital sums from investment spending large enough to cause a possibly irreversible collapse of the global capitalist system.

High-risk finance and an expansionist monetary policy allowed the US and the world to overcome the lowest point of the crisis and now allows Europe, plagued by the ordoliberalist austerity policy,[2] some breathing space because new financial capital expenditure in the Eurozone gives the financial illusion of new growth.

The problem remains that of worsening social disintegration: increasing inequality with low consumption keeps interest rates low and leads to low capital expenditure: everything interacts and overlaps.

European and German austerity policy is responsible for the rest; in other words, the constraints of balancing budgets—where they exist institutionally (only in Europe and for well-known structural reasons)—are a further incentive for cutting interest rates because they prevent new capital investment that could break the vicious cycle, that is, public spending for investment.

Yet this was the form of investment that was and is prevented in Europe, by pursuing a policy of social exclusion and attacking post-World War II welfare successes with a violence so far unprecedented in the history of capitalism.

The European and German deflationary policy is simply a monetary stamp of approval for the transformation—with its immense implications—imposed by the expanded capitalist accumulation cycle structure and its European institutions.

Public Spending and Social Reproduction: Overturning the Rhetoric

Huge problems will arise with social reproduction, which the entirely ideological debate on public debt, dominated by monetarist and deflationary thinking, prevents from progressing towards policies of full employment.

Only a return to a policy of full employment supported by public investments and measures to encourage private and public capital investment will reverse the trend, but the social impact will be enormous, and a cultural revolution will be required to overthrow nihilism and rampant injustice.

The first step in this cultural revolution is to overturn the prevailing discourse on public debt.

Reference to Michal Kalecki could help us here, particularly his article "Political Aspects of Full Employment".[3] This is a guiding star after years of wandering in the wilderness, and worth quoting in full here.

The essay states: "We shall deal first with the reluctance of the 'captains of industry' to accept government intervention in the matter of employment. Every widening of state activity is looked upon by business with suspicion, but the creation of employment by government spending has a special aspect which makes the opposition particularly intense.

Under a laissez-faire system, the level of employment depends to a great extent on the so-called state of confidence. If this deteriorates, private investment declines, which results in a fall of output and employment (both directly and through the secondary effect of the fall in incomes upon consumption and investment).

This gives the capitalists a powerful indirect control over government policy: everything which may shake the state of confidence must be carefully avoided because it would cause an economic crisis. But once the government learns the trick of increasing employment through its own investments, this powerful controlling device loses its effectiveness. Hence, budget deficits necessary to carry out government intervention must be regarded as perilous. The social function of the doctrine of 'sound finance' is to make the level of employment dependent on the state of confidence.

The dislike of business leaders for a government spending policy grows even more acute when they come to consider the objects on which the money would be spent: public investment and subsidising mass consumption.

The economic principles of government intervention require that public investment should be confined to objects which do not compete with the equipment of private business (e.g. hospitals, schools, highways). Otherwise, the profitability of private investment might be impaired, and the positive effect of public investment upon employment offset, by the negative effect of the decline in private investment.

This conception suits the businessmen very well. But the scope for public investment of this type is rather narrow, and there is a danger that the government, in pursuing this policy, may eventually be tempted to nationalise transport or public utilities to gain a new sphere for investment.[4]

One might, therefore, expect business leaders and their experts to be more in favour of subsidising mass consumption (by means of family allowances, subsidies to keep down the prices of necessities, etc.) than of public investment; for by subsidising consumption, the government would not be embarking on any sort of enterprise. In practice, however, this is not the case. Indeed, subsidising mass consumption is much more violently opposed by these experts than public investment.

For here, a moral principle of the highest importance is at stake. The fundamentals of capitalist ethics require that 'you shall earn your bread in sweat'—unless you happen to have private means".

Transformation of Public Intervention in the Crisis in the US and Japan

Today, the world faces the problem that capital gains in the form of income from very high-risk currency circulation have taken precedence over capitalist profits for approximately 30 years.

Capitalism has thus been "capitalised", not through inheritance of capital but by shifting huge masses of wealth from profit to financial income with the consequent very high-risk speculative bubbles.

Going back to Kalecki, the striking thing is that capitalist indignation with public intervention miraculously evaporated when the private debt of great universal capitalist banks, dispensers of financial instruments of mass destruction, had to be converted to sovereign debt, that is debt that all states had to shoulder—or securitised (playing for time before the crisis). Banks were even nationalised to prevent panic.

Any objection to public debt disappeared when the geopolitical leaders of global capitalist power came under scrutiny: the US and Japan are shining examples.

We only talk about public debt when the debtor nations are on the semi-periphery of central capital reproduction, such as Southern Europe, the Asian nations of the South China Sea and South-east Asia and South America.

Lack of growth and unemployment stemming from low productivity are conveniently not mentioned.

Legions of economists, some Nobel laureates, are falling over themselves to stress that the danger is not deflation but inflation (with rates below 2% in Europe: the unattainable goal of Mario Draghi's ruinous plan) and we must do anything to prevent it.

The ideological narrative of an intergenerational divide plays an interesting part in this economic and political debate. This assumes that a struggle is taking place between the generations and old people are beating young people with the stick of public debt. In this case, public debt is the budget deficit in resources accumulated by the state through taxation and savings accrued by the sacrifices of past, present and future generations in special reservoirs. There are as many types of reservoirs as there are different methods of allocating property rights, which the state or organisations determine to preserve savings or allocate them as forms of investment.

It is impossible for any state to constantly balance its budget.

The state, like the shifting economy, is constantly evolving, and budgetary balance is simply an illusion or an ideological tool to destroy public spending and public investments (which, as I said, assumes different forms of ownership), thus essentially destroying public spending in the strict sense and any form of non-community welfare.

This ideology, which lies at the root of ordoliberalist thinking, has become a very powerful and destructive instrument of European policy, as evidenced by the economic and social crisis of the last 20 years.

Instead of intergenerational conflict, we should be stressing the principle of citizenship, hard-won after decades of struggle by workers and the mutually supportive culture of many segments of the international bourgeoisie, aware that there can be no growth without social peace and therefore without social cohesion.

The European Exception to the Generational Narrative

This ideological and symbolic phenomenon must be strongly emphasised, particularly in Europe.[5]

According to European rhetoric, deflation is low inflation, and the abstract variable of budgetary balance is treated as a concrete means of ensuring economic growth. Anyone with any knowledge of the history of economic thought—and we are dwindling in number—understands that the practice of hypostatisation (treating or representing something abstract as a concrete reality) stems from the French monetarist school of the 1930s led by Jacques Rueff, who was leading advocate of a return to the gold standard.

The strong Franc and military power were meant to bolster France in its ambitions to dominate Europe and even challenge the US. General De Gaulle, with his *force de frappe*, was known to be a great champion of this policy.

Even though no-one had any time for this paradigm, and it was discarded during the first steps towards European policy (with an avalanche of public interventions and public debt), this hoary Hegelian approach ended up laying the ground for the structure of Europe and all the European states until German unification, beginning with the near-Soviet agricultural policy.

Then British insular reluctance to give up their currency (let us keep the pound), Italian lack of financial nous and French imperial magniloquence led to the dusting off of an idea popularised by Rueff.[6] This was used to give credence to the German dream of unifying itself and all of Europe around a Deutschmark that, unlike the Franc, was so strong that it could masquerade as a Euro and generate a trade surplus for Germany (which now had 80 million inhabitants!) that would make all the other European countries quake in their boots.

The French dream turned into the nightmare that the Germans continue to impose on all Europe—the trade surplus, strong currency, ever-increasing productivity, wage increases and reduced public spending. Now everyone in Europe is having to sing to Germany's tune—and like it or lump it.

Deficit and Debt

We all know that there is a difference between public deficit and debt.

Debt builds up in years of deficit. Annual deficits come about for a range of reasons: trade deficit instead of surplus, tax revenues failing to offset expenditure, low economic growth preventing the scope of taxation from being extended and so on.

The difference between deficit and budget introduces a time factor and this forces even those who believe in a permanently balanced economy to think in evolutionary or historical terms. Having to sing to the German tune means that history has been interpreted over the last quarter of a century by ignoring every difference between deficit and debt and above all by ignoring the causes feeding deficit and hence debt.

Everything has been done to make people forget class differences in society.

Agrippa Menenius Lanatus used the analogy of body parts to argue that plebs and patricians are mutually dependent. One cannot survive without the other. Everything must be in harmony for health, peace and prosperity.

One hand washes the other. Now Agrippa Menenius Lanatus's parable has been replaced by the parable of the old killing the new. There is something bizarre about this. In a monetary economy such as a capitalist economy, where people are tangible commodities, economic structures suddenly became personalised and led to the idea of a struggle between young and old.

We hear stories in Europe that we do not hear anywhere else in the world: "Younger generations should not have to pay for the failures of the old. Every baby is born with a public debt burden of several thousand euro". If these nursery rhymes were told in the US and Japan, everyone would laugh, particularly the politicians who are very careful not to upset their electorate and lose votes from any generations.

To support the fable of intergenerational conflict over public debt, we would first have to answer the question asked by the great Karl Mannheim,[7] about whether generations really exist and are not a purely statistical convention designed to put some order in the world.

Christian personalists, for example, would never fall into this trap because they know that everyone is the way they are because they are always unique, reproducible and irreplaceable.

In the words of Ranke: "Everyone is alone before God".

But I digress: now such arguments no longer interest anyone.

However, as I will discuss later, we still need to distinguish between public debt for public spending and public debt for public waste. Those who support good public spending are the leading opponents of public waste. There is also some truth in the belief that at certain stages of high-risk monetary circulation cycles—where state borrowing becomes toxic instead of normal—an increase in public debt can make public deficit grow even faster. In this case, the effects can be disastrous, imposing (in an open economy) truly toxic levels of unproductive state expenditure to face an increase, for example, in government bond yields, thus preventing states from acting on social cohesion (particularly when growth is very low) and causing a debt spiral that is difficult to break.

Low Growth, Demographics, Labour: Problems to Be Solved

To regain a certain awareness of being and understand our economic and social situation in Europe, we must begin to dismantle the misleading ideology of public debt as an intergenerational struggle.

Only by doing so can we truly raise hopes for new generations currently crippled by very high unemployment and the crisis in the educational system.

If we compare public expenditure in different European countries, we can see that Italy has one of the lowest levels. This essentially means that deficits, and therefore debt, are a product of low economic growth and the first factor of this economic growth is inherent to the demographic problem, because this underlies the intergenerational relationship: population employment levels are the problem.

Throughout the world, these are unequal but always very low. More people, therefore, start working later and stop working sooner than they used to in "advanced" nations.

The working population has been shrinking for centuries instead of expanding, but this has not led to an increase in work productivity. The outcome has been a fall in investments and a decline in the likelihood of investing in the expectation of profit, adding up to a national picture of low competitiveness.

If we fail to expand the working population and ensure a stable, growing profit rate trend, we will not be able to extend the tax revenue base and will, therefore, have fewer public and private resources for tackling and resolving the infrastructure costs that accompany growth.

This leads to a collapse in "total factory productivity", which measures the productivity of labour as well as the efficiency of the complex systems that generate the material wealth of nations, thus determining their different positions on the world productivity scale.

Social Reproduction Is Difficult

It is easy to see that any complex system, such as a society with tens of millions of inhabitants, needs infrastructure to produce and reproduce social cycles. If production generates low growth and low tax revenues, public debt increases, and social reproduction becomes very difficult because it is configured asymmetrically in relation to needs and the funding required to meet those needs.

Let us consider the fact that minimum relational needs must be satisfied for social reproduction, or society will break down into a Hobbesian state of nature. If these needs cannot be met through economic growth that generates public spending without deficit and without debt, they are met by lowering growth, leading to bigger deficits and thus debt.

The alternative to the above solution is the destruction of society, as was politically attempted in Greece by the deflationary European "Troika", which set out to destroy the Greek social system and ultimately that of Europe.

This has been only partially successful due to the stability of the political system and the strong traditionalist roots that society has maintained intact (extended family, guiding role of the elderly and so on). The welfare state has been replaced with a natural and associative unified, community-based system.

Party machinery and the political system are also intrinsic to public expenditure and public debt, in the sense of increasing parasitic earnings engendered by two-way or group political cronyism (the nations of Southern Europe and South America are a classic international example),[8] but also of showing that a properly institutionalised political system, that is, independent of civil society and its degenerations, can play a positive role in doing away with rent-seeking behaviour—in other words, expenditure that is not public spending but public waste.

European Growth Is Possible Only If the Public Debt Paradigm Changes

Admittedly, Europe continues to be an economic giant but one with feet of clay. The contraction is still going on: domestic markets are shrinking due to a colossal shift of wealth from labour to capital exacerbated by anti-grassroots free-market counter-reforms of the labour market, a harbinger of unemployment and not employment, mainly brought about the political Left, all too often supported by fawning trade unions. This leads to a collapse in investments and the European Central Bank (ECB), which is created on the model of the Bundesbank and not the Federal Reserve System (FED): in other words, a federal bank for a federal continent and thus able to govern different productivity rates, and different trade deficits cannot stand up properly to the deflationary German hegemony. This policy, dictated by an ideological fundamentalism that fetishises public debt, is killing off European growth and development.

This is why changing the view of public debt is a common theme throughout our political and cultural debate.

Public waste should not be confused with public spending, which is currently the only way to relaunch investment and employment, along with community and subsidiary economy. If we fail to do this, Europe will become a falling star and the workers will be first to pay the price.

The decline and political dwarfing of Europe by German hegemony is reflected by the absence of a European role in the Mediterranean tragedies, its absence in world diplomacy and the decline of the cultural, humanistic life, which was always its beating heart.

We can only reverse this march and envisage a Europe of growth and development if we reform European representation: in other words, if we give power to Parliament and not the unelected Commission, which vetoes any voted-in law that is not a carbon copy of its Directives.

We also need to reform European representative institutions to make room for organised labour and therefore trade union forces, redesigning the profile of a unified continent underpinned by the sharing of sovereignty between nations and not between functional segments intent on doing away with unification such as those under German rule. National plans should be shared to achieve the dream of a United States of Europe with a strong social bias.

Europe Is the Epicentre of Deflation and Power Imbalance

The last ten years of world history have been characterised by what David Calleo calls "power's follies",[9] in other words a presumption by the US that it can rule the world by itself.

After the fall of the USSR, the three families who brought the greatest world power to its knees—the Clinton, Bush and Obama families—were all united by two beliefs, which dominated their actions.

Their lives were also materially supported by the first belief, that is the universal and beneficial dominant role of finance at the expense of industry and services.

The second belief was that the world order could be guaranteed by the American republic alone.

The most telling and naive expression of this doctrine was Obama's famous interview with *The Atlantic*.[10]

Obama clearly signalled his imperial designs by aiming to do what not even Charles V succeeded in doing on the Atlantic shores, through a plan masterfully described by Federico Chabod in *Carlo V° e lo stato di Milano*,[11] that is, uniting the Spanish Empire from the Potosi mines to the Netherlands, with Milan as its archetypal point.

In the end, the Milanese aristocracy did not even manage to establish a territorial state, whereas Venice extended as far as Lodi. Obama wanted to go one better: establish the archetypal point in Washington and unite the European and Asian dominions with two trade treaties that would assure world domination for the US.

This plan had two colossal weaknesses.

The Trans-Pacific Partnership excluded China and we all saw how that ended: with the rise of Neo-Maoism under Xi Jinping.

The EU did not sign the Trans-Pacific Partnership due to interstate conflicts within the Union and the result was the flimsy Canada-EU Comprehensive Economic and Trade Agreement (CETA), which remains to be approved by individual European national parliaments.

After the collapse of the USSR, it is becoming increasingly clear that it will be impossible to piece together a new system of international balance able to face the threat of a global nuclear war as is the case when international relations are balanced and ordered: there are fewer, moderated conflicts between nations and uneven local "variable geometry" conflicts when the overriding aim is to prevent world destruction by an atomic bomb.

This situation has come about because the collapse of the USSR was not followed by a new Yalta Conference or a new Congress of Vienna: the *Empereur* may have been a more fearful *monstre* than Stalinism, but the restorers of absolutist order treated France as the great power as it still was and accorded it the dignity of being part of the *Entente Cordiale*, which lasted until the Congress of Berlin in 1885.

Nothing like this happened with the fall of the USSR apart from failure to comply with the gentleman's agreement Gorbachev and Reagan shook hands on: in other words, that no nation bordering the former USSR, now Russia, should belong to NATO or the EU.

The three families did entirely the opposite, caught up in the folly of their unipolar dream, which only crumbled with the outbreak of the Mesopotamian crisis and the decisive intervention in Putin's Russian conflict.

Trump's election is simply a sign that the North American people are having the first inklings that they cannot dominate the world on their own.

China's advent in the international arena, which has been going on for about a decade, should have been enough to tell them that the dream was impossible. Leaving such a long period without a new international agreement reflecting the need for renewed cooperation between world powers was bound to have consequences.

I believe that this awareness stems, paradoxically, from two great mistakes made during the history of humankind.

Because we are not absolutist historians or Hegelians who believe that reality is always rational, we are bound to concur that Trump's election was a tragedy arising out of the colossal mistakes made by the North American ruling classes and the reaction that followed when people were given a chance to vote democratically.

We all know the reasons for this reaction: rebellion by people cast into the abyss due to financial deindustrialisation; forms of labour that amount to modern slavery; a crisis in the middle classes due to unequal world capitalist accumulation leading to migratory flows—and the ensuing global cultural and anthropological clashes, with conflicts between African and Eurasian peoples that have repercussions in Europe.

The second mistake was made when the European Union was created under the influence of Jean Monnet's functionalist theories.[12]

These theories make it possible to avoid having to choose between federalism and confederalism, because they remove areas of sovereignty from nation states unbeknownst to their citizens: the ruling political classes collaborate in the functionalist construct like a new comprador bourgeoisie and share the technocratic plan of supranational expropriation.[13]

This comes about because they intersect, through growing industrial and financial internationalisation, with the cosmopolitan transnational bourgeoisie, who are engaged in an ongoing relationship of osmosis and mingling with the internal bourgeoisie.[14]

This begins before members of the bourgeoisie even rise to the upper echelons of international power: it begins during the increasingly internationalised education experienced by the children of the bourgeoisie. They may be completely international or only internal and comprador and simultaneously internal, depending on the internationalisation cycles to which nation states are subject and the generational life-cycle in which the personal fortunes of the bourgeoisie are caught up.

The incubators of this bourgeoisie began on a European scale, unsurprisingly led by the most international territorial and national area comprising Benelux, France and Germany, which are engaged in a constantly unstable balance of power.

Italy was part of it, always as an unstable vassal state. The US followed this process, alternately encouraging it (via conflict with the USSR) or fearing the outcome (due to weakening of the transatlantic and military ties that could arise).

The setting up of the European Common Market in 1957 saw the establishment of a *Zollverein* protected on the outside by heavy customs barriers but with free circulation of goods and people inside. The first great functionalist European Union policy began to be introduced, with the start of the technocrat-led Common Agricultural Policy. Power thus began to devolve from national parliaments to a technocracy that I define as mixed because it arose out of a Europe-wide mixture of meritocratic and party-based decisions.[15]

In the wake of that policy, the collapse of the USSR led to the Franco-German agreement, with Italy again participating as a vassal state. This brought the single currency into existence as well as a fixed currency exchange rate system governed by a European central bank modelled on the Bundesbank.

The agreement foreshadowed the irreconcilable European contradiction: it is impossible to hold together a fixed-exchange single currency system that prevents competitive devaluations typical of flexible exchange systems (if not by resorting to internal devaluation), when the nation states involved have different overall productivity rates. This is the case in Europe and has led to high structural unemployment, growing poverty and marked inequalities in a strongly deflationary context.

How did this happen?

It came about because of another folly of power: Europe incorporates different socioeconomic constructs, as I discussed in a work dating from 1994,[16] when I predicted that such a system could not work except at huge social cost attended by dramatic plunges in fixed capital stock asset production.

All this was made even more evident by the German cultural hegemony, which became manifest in the Maastricht and subsequent Agreements.

In their age-old struggle with France, the Germans felt they had to establish the supremacy of their own national economic system.

This was possible only through the general application, within the fabric of European bureaucracy and technocracy, of the principles of *ordoliberismus* as consecrated in a work by Walter Eucken entitled *Die Nationale Ökonomie.*[17] Although based on very flimsy theory, its simplicity made it perfect for propaganda purposes. It led to the undeserved prominence of social market economy, which Wilhelm Röpke[18] theorised about on even flimsier grounds in works that are unfortunately read to this day.

The basic premise of *ordoliberismus* is the abstract notion that it is possible to achieve a state without debt and perennially low deficit in a world without capitalist cycles and with equal levels of territorial and national productivity, coupled with Robinson's free-market principle. Human communities failing to achieve this are relegated to perennial subalternity.[19]

In other words, weak subaltern nation states are linked by technocratic and oligarchical functionalist ties in a master-slave relationship to a state or states enjoying a trade surplus due to higher national productivity and the importation of low-cost goods.

In common parlance, this is referred to as a relationship between creditor states and debtor states, where the relationship between states is commoditised and set out like a double-entry ledger!

This is the situation in Europe today, with Germany at the centre and France as its subaltern.

France and Germany

France could hardly remain silent when faced with this situation of German domination over Europe, wielded through technocracy and economic power.

More than other nations, France needs a domestic and foreign policy that restores its balance of power in relation to the European oligarchies and the US due to possession of the atom bomb and because its position in NATO is different from that of other European nations.

Europe will reflect the crux of transalpine foreign policy, an increasingly essential issue, but with a different emphasis as compared to the 2008 economic crisis, in the context of a deflationary crisis that is destined to become permanent.[20]

In years to come, the French international, comprador bourgeoisie will certainly not turn their backs on Europe but will think much more about looking after affairs in their African empire. Their real interest lies in dominating the mechanism of expanding capitalist accumulation in northern and sub-Saharan Africa and particularly in Mesopotamia, where an economic reconstruction boom like that experienced in France and Germany after World War II will begin once the war with ISIS is over.

This is why it is essential to be in on the final throes of the current international war, particularly in Syria (as we have seen with Russia), because Syria is increasingly strategic to the new international power struggles in the area.

France and Germany are bound to maintain a good relationship with Russia, despite North American pressure.

Germany's global military presence is weak due to its history[21] even though it is a dominant nation in Europe.

In any case, the dog is biting its own tail: *ordoliberismus* forces all semi-federal and semi-Confederate states to curtail military expenditure for European budgetary reasons. On the Syrian front, the French role is somewhat understated due to budgetary problems (this is amazing considering the history of Francophone ties in Syria and Lebanon and the Maronite and Alawite roots of French domination). Military expenditure is cut, and this is another reason why France is against a policy of austerity decided only by the Germans.

In short, it is difficult for France to regain the power it once wielded with the Assad family (its own creation) in this war-torn Middle Eastern country.

The same is true for Libya.

Paris will, therefore, try to make up for lost ground in Syria[22] by establishing a further presence in sub-Saharan Africa and will forge tighter links with the Gulf countries, placing itself in continuous competition with Italy.

Relations between the US and France will not be easy in this scenario, but this is nothing new.

The French Revolution marked the pinnacle of their cooperation. The anti-British revolutionaries found a loyal ally in the French and this marked a milestone in the world thought with a triad formed by Edmund Burke, the founding fathers with all their differences and European choices between confederalists and federalists. But those days are long gone.

In the 1920s and 1930s, the US and France were potential architects of a pan European scenario strongly anchored to US military might and North American major finance, as evidenced by the personal stories of Aristide Briand and Jean Monnet.

After World War II, De Gaulle changed France and international relations with the weakening of NATO and the birth, even among the French reformist Left, of a combined spirit of autonomist revenge and economic competition, as reflected by the title of the masterpiece by Jean-Jacques Servan-Schreiber: *Le defi americaine.*

The international bourgeoisie came under violent attack by the more comprador and nationalist bourgeoisie, and international relations immediately suffered.

Even then, Germany was the problem. In an uninterrupted chain of events after De Gaulle, the Élysée and leading French industries interpreted the confrontation with the US from the viewpoint of a hegemonic European nation integrated under the Franco-British hegemony.

France and the US regarded one another as superpowers, naturally with great differences in volume and influence, but this comparison guaranteed that France could aim for hegemony in Europe due to its good relations with Russia.[23]

The collapse of the USSR and consequent German unification was a tragedy for the French: they lost European hegemony and their good relations with Russia—ruthlessly humiliated by the US—were not enough to save them. Macron, a neo-Gaullist, rocked in a different cradle from the one that nurtured Jean Monnet and Aristide Briands, is now playing his neo-nationalist card by stepping up his relations with the US to increase his bargaining position and power with Germany, whose economy is increasingly anti-US.

This is an irony of history: now it is up to Germany to support the balance of European power and extend it to Africa, which we would be wrong to consider only in terms of migration.

In the long run, Africa will offer the same rewards as the reconstruction of Libya and Mesopotamia will do in the extremely short term.

Germany and France will take up position on Syria and the Maghreb, in competition with Trump, and France will naturally have the historical edge over other Europeans.

Trump will always play an essential part, even if he is oblivious to it. We need the US to stop global international relations descending into anarchy. The US cannot escape this role, whether it likes it or not.

Neo-colonialism and Neo-imperialism

As we continue to explore the concept of international relations, we can hardly overlook the fact that the burgeoning new capitalism, based on an impressive set of technological and proprietary forces, is at its heart a world power system built on fault lines of dependency between nations and between classes, as explained by Emanuele Wallenstein[24] and Samir Amin.[25]

Amin sets out the best case. Taking Marx's writings on non-European societies as his starting point, he formulates a theory of transition to a capitalist economy in underdeveloped regions. The process of creating surplus value in peripheral economies and social constructs involves an unequal exchange that is translated into processes of indebtedness affecting peripheral countries (essentially due to returns on foreign investment in countries of the South). This comes about because, as in the past, the model of transition to peripheral capitalism is essentially different from that of transition to central capitalism. Commercial aggression from the outside imposed by capitalist production methods on pre-capitalistic constructs involves some crucial regressive social processes, such as the decline of the craft industry, which is not replaced by local industrial production. The contemporary agricultural crisis in the developing world is to a large extent the consequence of these breakdown processes. Foreign capital investment is no remedy, because the aim of industries set up in the periphery is to extract resources. An unequal international specialisation of labour manifests itself in specifically configured forms of capitalist accumulation that arise in peripheral nations. The prevalence of activities involving the export of raw materials and unfinished manufactured products, together with processes to assemble high-tech goods built in nations central to world accumulation, is not dependent upon the inadequacy of the domestic market but on the centre's productive superiority in all fields. This relegates the periphery to the role of supplementary supplier of products in which it boasts a natural advantage: exotic agricultural products and mining products. When this distortion leads to the remuneration of work on the periphery becoming lower than that prevailing at the centre for the same productivity, industries targeting the peripheral domestic market are allowed limited growth, while trade becomes unequal.

The next model of industrialisation to replace imports and the still-embryonic model of the new international division of labour within a multinational enterprise cannot change the essential conditions of this process, which I define as "extraversion", even though forms of capital accumulation continue to change.[26]

This distortion leads to the expansion of the service sector at the periphery, which cannot be justified by growth in the demand structure or in productivity. In global centres of capitalist accumulation, this expansion reflects difficulties in achieving surplus value inherent in the advanced monopolistic stage, as Bara and Sweezy have shown,[27] while at the periphery it stems from limits and contradictions typical of peripheral development from the outset: inadequate industrialisation and growing unemployment, strengthening of the ground rent position. This expansion in unproductive activities, which halts accumulation and manifests itself particularly in expanding administrative expenditure, leads to an almost permanent public finance meltdown in the contemporary developing world. Unequal international specialisation also lies at the root of another skewing in favour of "light" productive activity sectors, in which modern production techniques such as *maquiladoras* are adopted.[28]

This skewing determines a peripheral growth pattern different from that historically followed by the West.

An analysis of strategies adopted by foreign monopolies in underdeveloped countries shows that the underdeveloped country lacks the economic means to take the upper hand until the prevailing dogma that the periphery must always be assimilated by the dominant market is called into question.

Unregulated financialisation has further fed this dependency, primarily by acting on the phenomenon of securitising public debt and profits derived by centres of accumulation from inflationary processes that destroy national fixed capital in the periphery and encourage dependency, as deflation does in the capitalist centre of a united Europe, as I have demonstrated previously.

Underdevelopment is manifest not in per capita production but in specific structural characteristics, such as the huge inequalities typical of production distribution at the periphery within the price system determined by the centre. These inequalities stem from the nature of peripheral constructs and determine much of the income distribution structure.

This situation is exacerbated by the disjointedness caused at the periphery by production being oriented in a direction consistent with the needs of the centre. This prevents the benefits of economic progress being transferred from development hubs to the economic organisation with financing structures being typically dependent on growth in the periphery according to the dynamics of foreign financial capital accumulation.

As the economy grows in the periphery, this accentuated underdevelopment finds its necessary outlet in preventing growth.

In other words, however much per capita production is achieved, it is impossible to move to a situation where growth is self-centred and self-driven.

While the capitalist means of production tends to become exclusive in the centre, this does not happen in the periphery, where constructs are therefore essentially different from those in the centre. Their forms depend on the nature of the pre-capitalistic constructs from which they stem and on how and when they became part of the global system. This explains the essential difference between peripheral constructs and young, central constructs based on the dominance of a simple mercantile means of production, which contain the embryonic potential to develop into an established capitalist means of production. Whatever the initial differences, peripheral constructs tend to adhere to a model characterised by the dominance of agricultural and commercial capital dependent on foreign organisations (*comprador*). The domination of central capital over the system, and the essential primary accumulation mechanisms, established for its benefit, into which this domination translates, impose limits on the development of national capitalism that ultimately depend on political relationships.

The debilitated national society in the periphery confers an apparent specific weight on local bureaucracy and determines functions that are different from those typical of bureaucratic and technocratic social bodies in the centre. Contradictions inherent in the onset of underdevelopment and the rise of the petit bourgeois strata reflecting these contradictions, explain the current trend towards state capitalism. This new way of developing capitalism in the periphery is not a means of transition towards socialism but expresses future ways of organising new relationships between the centre and periphery.

Michael Kalecki is essential reading in this regard.[29]

He characterises a range of new regimes in decolonised developing countries—from Nehru's India and Nasser's Egypt to Sukarno's Indonesia—as "intermediate regimes". Here, the "intermediate class" (or *petit bourgeoisie*)—occupying the social space between capitalists and workers and comprising the middle class in urban areas and the peasantry in rural areas—wields state power.

The *petit bourgeoisie* has never wielded state power in history, he argued. Whenever its representatives chanced to come to power, they "invariably served the interests of big business (often allied with the remnants of the feudal system)". But a *dénouement* where they wielded State power on their own became possible in the particular conjuncture following decolonisation for two specific reasons: one internal and one external.

The internal reason was the country's colonial past, which had stunted the growth of the bourgeoisie proper and correspondingly of the proletariat. The external reason was the existence of the Soviet Union and the socialist bloc on the one side, and of the US and the capitalist world on the other, between whom the intermediate regime could manoeuvre to get aid without too many strings, and to prevent any pressure to move towards either classical capitalism or classical socialism. Kalecki saw the intermediate regime as a durable phenomenon, whose two main features were state capitalism—that is, an emphasis on the public sector, and on non-alignment.

Kalecki's theory has been much discussed and much criticised. Whether these regimes, even as they were at the time, could be characterised as intermediate regimes with *petit bourgeois* hegemony, or whether they were regimes dominated by the bourgeoisie which only used the public sector as a means of developing capitalism, as the Communist Parties in countries like India argued, was one point of controversy. The other related to its alleged durability. Indeed, within a few years of Kalecki's writing, Egypt under Anwar Sadat and Indonesia under Suharto (whose accession to power was accompanied by a massacre of communists) had already moved away from his picture of an intermediate regime. One point, however, where Kalecki was certainly right was the social and political weight of the intermediate class or *petit bourgeoisie* in the ex-colonial Third World countries. The question, therefore, arises: how do we trace the subsequent history of this intermediate class in India?

The Nehruvian *dirigiste* regime had got into a crisis long before economic liberalisation—starting in the mid-1980s and gathering momentum in the 1990s—supplanted it. The proximate reason for the crisis is not far to seek. Given the importance of the State as an economic player within that regime, growing public expenditure was crucial for sustaining the growth process under it. But its capacity to raise fiscal resources to keep such expenditure going atrophied progressively, primarily because of the resistance of the capitalists, and the rich in general, to pay taxes. (India was and remains, to this day, a country with one of the lowest ratios of tax revenue to national income anywhere in the world.) Inevitably, therefore, what ensued was a combination of inflation, caused by excessive government borrowing, indirect taxes and a slackening of growth, and with it of the growth rate of employment, which inter alia alienated urban middle-class support from it.

The crisis of the *dirigiste* regime began from the mid-1960s, though the Green Revolution—for which bank nationalisation and the introduction of directed credit towards agriculture was an important contributory factor—gave it a transitory reprieve. The crisis of unemployment afflicting the urban middle class, captured so tellingly in Mrinal Sen's film, *Chorus*, radicalised it greatly. This was manifest in some parts of India in the support for the movement led by Jaya Prakash Narayan, and in other parts, especially in West Bengal, in its moving closer to the Left.

The Left's inability to move centre-stage, for which it was best positioned just before Indira Gandhi's assassination in 1984, together with international developments, including the emergence of the phenomenon of globalized finance and the subsequent collapse of the Soviet Union, opened the way for the supplanting of Nehruvian *dirigisme* not by any alternative proposed by the Left, but by the neo-liberal trajectory of development. What neo-liberalism has done, however, is to bring about a schism between the peasantry and the urban middle class, the two major components of Kalecki's intermediate class. The peasantry has been, quite clearly, a victim of neo-liberal policies, which have entailed a withdrawal of State support from it, expressed, among other things, in the dwindling of institutional credit to peasant agriculture and the re-emergence of private moneylending in new forms. Not surprisingly, per capita food grains availability for all uses has declined to a level no higher than what it had been in the years before World War II (aided also by government holding of excessive stocks and the export of food grains). At the same time, important segments of the urban middle class have been beneficiaries of the neo-liberal regime,

> which explains their desire for the so-called "development" identified with neo-liberalism. It is a symptom of the schism between the peasantry and this segment of the urban middle class that the Left's attempt to relate to this segment by pursuing the development agenda, as it is currently understood, alienated from it the support of sections of the peasantry in its one-time bastion, West Bengal.
>
> The neo-liberal trajectory itself, however, has *now* run into a crisis, characterised by slowing growth, acute inflation, absolute stagnation in manufacturing output, growing unemployment (camouflaged as rising informal, temporary and intermittent employment), dwindling opportunities for large segments of the urban middle class and an extremely precarious balance-of-payments situation that can get into a tail-spin with the tapering off of the "quantitative easing" being pursued by the Federal Reserve Board of the US (which is pumping huge amounts of liquidity into the world economy). The crisis of the neo-liberal trajectory is, once again, alienating large sections of the urban middle class from the current economic regime.[30]

Financialised global capitalism now faces the challenge of reconstruction on these fragile social bases, aptly encapsulated by the hegemonic difficulties that pervade Indian capitalism and, to an even greater extent, monopolistic difficulties faced by the dictatorial Chinese state. The deep-seated US crisis, as we have already discussed, harbours an inability to reconstruct a new international system that incorporates "intermediate regimes" now focusing on growth in a new balance of power.

We need a new balance of power, as I will discuss later—a new system of international capitalism, between European deflation and the emergence from post-colonial dependence that is bound to involve re-establishing old conceptual models. Bertrand Badie summarised this superbly in his latest work, when he wrote: "Une science de l'international n'est plus concevable ajourd'hui sans ..l' effort de reconstruction patient et froid de la subjectivité des tous les acteurs, touchant, en priorité, ceux qui relèvent d'une autre histoire. C'est ce que la vieille science politique tenait pour inutile et peut-étre poétique, ce que la culture westphalienne prenait pour folklorique et ce que l'école du choix rationnel considère toujours comme hors de propos. Les trois, face au monde tel qu'il est aujourd'hui, divers et intersubjectif, ont totalement failli."[31]

This failure is more serious if we think of capitalism as a social form of world production. Globalism forces even those who think that Say's law rules the world, that is, that supply creates its own demand, to see things as they are really are: a planetary socioeconomic construct that gradually forces all pre-capitalistic socioeconomic constructs into submission.

Rosa Luxemburg had this very concept of capitalism as a global socio-economic construct in mind when she wrote *Accumulation of capital* and her "Anti-Critique"[32]: *an extraordinarily contemporary thought*[33] *because it does not shy from discussing the general nature of the mechanism of penetration and development of capitalist accumulation alongside* the *specificities* of the various processes by which capitalist markets penetrate non-capitalist societies: the struggle of capital against the natural economy—and the struggle against a simple mercantile economy. All this is going on at the same time as the global competitive struggle between capitals to grab the remaining accumulation possibilities. We are now witnessing full penetration of international financial capital: North American and European financial capitals are exerting a gravitational pull on the economic life of all emerging countries, with the trap of public debt and the military expenditure and infrastructures feeding the debt, offering further possibilities for achieving surplus value and a kind of interstate regulation of world accumulation.

This capitalism has been joined in recent decades by Chinese monopolistic capitalism based on a bureaucratic and terrorist dictatorship, whose role is increasingly like the historically established part played by "Western" capitalism.

This role was admirably described by David Pilling in an article published in the "Financial Times", which is much better theoretically argued than many academic papers: "Many African governments have gone on Eurobond borrowing sprees, meaning they are in debt as much to Wall Street and the City of London as to Beijing. Researchers at Johns Hopkins found that only in Zambia, Djibouti and possibly Congo-Brazzaville were loans from Beijing the major cause of debt distress. If China is weaponising capital—using loans to create countries in its own image—then the west did the same in the 1970s and 1980s when it made massive and unsustainable loans to Africa through multilateral institutions such as the World Bank and IMF. When those loans turned sour, the same institutions pushed through their favourite medicine: hated structural adjustment programmes that eviscerated the state—and from which many countries are arguably still recovering. Certainly, there have been problems with Chinese finance too. Angola's government took over last year only to find that loans made under the previous regime to Sonangol, the state oil company, were far more expensive than advertised.

Chinese financed projects often lack strict environmental safeguards and can be shoddy."[34]

The 19th Chinese Communist Party Congress of autumn 2017 offered more acute observers an insight into the Chinese state's long-term monopolistic capitalist strategy in the context of international power relationships. The very long historical trading slump that began in the mid-1400s—when Zheng He, a great Chinese navigator of Muslim origin, was called back to his homeland by a fading Emperor to have his Navy destroyed—is finally over. That was how the impassable barrier between China and the rest of the world that lasted until the nineteenth-century opium wars was put up.

The Middle Empire, surrounded by barbarians, dominated the situational powers for centuries, effectively secluded by their immense lands. The great international experts on China, from Needham[35] to Gernet,[36] racked their brains for decades to define the triggering cause of that retreat from the barbarian world at a time when China had such immense power.

Xi Jinping is the resolution of an enigma. China is going back to what it used to be in its imperial heyday: a great power reaching out for world domination. It is doing this by staking its hopes on a thinker who supported the idea of internal control as a source of expansion abroad: good old Wittfogwel,[37] proponent of the "Asiatic mode of production". This paradigm is based on strict Imperial domination of the potentates who controlled the waters and hence the Empire: internal control of the sources of power was necessary to achieve this end.

Mao tried to achieve that control but at a huge social cost. The cultural revolution was simply a way to annihilate the opposing factions of a party that from the outset had to come to terms with Japanese nationalism followed by rivalry with Stalin and the international might of the Soviet Union, following the stamping out of revolt and strikes in Shanghai in

1927. China's enemies were not only at home: behind its back, the great Soviet power had created North Korea to ensure that China had to beg for help from the Soviets against Japan and then the US to ensure its very existence.

Mao put down his adversaries physically and morally until his death. Then Den Xiaoping was able to emerge and establish the rule consensually respected by the warring factions until Xi Jinping's rise to power: bureaucrats had to stop killing each another. The same thing happened in the Soviet Union with the advent of Khrushchev.

Xi Jinping broke the rule as soon as he came to power, gradually stepping up his fight against corruption and thus confirming in practice what everyone in the world knows in theory from decades studying the topic: the war on corruption is nothing more than a blunt instrument wielded in the internal struggle between power élites; the degree of bloodletting depends on the type of democratic legitimacy in force at any given time.

China is one of the least civilised human settlements from a judicial viewpoint: this can be understood provided the situation is dealt with scientifically and not to derive economic advantage, as with its admission to the WTO. The US Democratic Party led by the higher echelons of unregulated finance gave the green light for this and thus laid the foundations for the global catastrophe in which we are now mired.

The history is linear: when Xi Jinping rose to power in 2012, he shared it with very active factions associated with his immediate predecessors: Hu Jintao and Jiang Zemin. However, Xi broke with the rules of collegial control imposed by Deng. He rapidly took control of the Military Commission, which is nothing unusual, but then went on to secure Internal Security and Economy.

Xi gradually laid the foundations for a new expert, trusted faction at home and abroad, paving his way beyond the Middle Empire with no fear of internal enemies.

Strategic security of China's borders with Russia is crucial if China under the "new emperor" is to achieve the dazzling expansion it desires. This process cannot go ahead without agreement with Russia, following the roadmap laid by the Shanghai conferences: the new pact can unite China, Russia and India, allowing Beijing to continue its dominion of the seas, conceived in accordance with the ideas of Alfred Thayer Mahan,[38] that is, a geopolitical vision based on sea power taught in the US Navy schools.

It is vital to bring the North Korean crisis to an end. Stalin invented North Korea with the intention of scaring Japan and weakening Mao to force him to seek help from the Soviets in the event of war with the US. Those days are long gone, but cooperation between the US, Russia and China means that the issue could be resolved by annihilating the North Korean leadership—which would involve many more victims than the inner circle of leadership. It is an inevitable choice, because Xi Jinping has drawn a line representing the cyclical expansion of China's overseas presence. Now that the internal front has been stabilised, foreign conquests will strengthen China from within and vice versa. This will increase territorial conflict with India, the Philippines and especially Vietnam, China's age-old enemy.

These conflicts will decide the fate of strategic nations like Thailand (which has never been colonised in its history) that are understandably strengthening their military regimes, as happening in all of Indochina. Once the South Seas hinterland is secured, China can strike out to conquer Africa and Australia from Djibouti.

Reflecting on the history of the Chinese Communist Party, I often recognise in Xi's slogans the words not of Mao but of Liu Shaoqi,[39] who pursued a typically Soviet quest for social legitimisation of "red bureaucracy" through technological and military conquest, strictly controlling party cadres and developing global power in the international arena.

This is confirmed by the recent clamp-down on Chinese universities, which are called upon to foster "Chinese ideology" and improve their facilities to ensure fewer and fewer Chinese students leave China to study abroad.

Xi Jinping's secret is to expand as a great power in the world but return to the wellspring of national power. If he wins, a completely new system of global power and relevance will arise. The resulting form of capitalism will face growing economic, political and military conflict.

Historical needs for fierce global rivalry around premises for the accumulation of capital are ultimately a first-class breeding ground for capital accumulation. The more energetically capitalism assimilates the means of production and labour forces of countries and societies that are not completely capitalist (these days, through post-colonial politics), the more capital reproduction works within capitalist countries to remove a growing percentage of purchasing power from non-capitalist strata of the country of origin and from the working class.

This is evidenced by the growing relative impoverishment, which is now clear to everyone.

The obsolete term "imperialism" has even disappeared from the vocabulary of the Left, to be replaced by the more aseptic "globalisation", which apparently alludes to a natural and peaceful process of market expansion. The term may have fallen into disuse, but imperialism, conceived as an aggressive intertwining of economic and military powers that enhances the world's inequalities, is very much alive today.

New Areas of State: Between Leviathan and Behemoth

Given the global failure of neo-liberalism, we need to rethink the idea of State, bearing in mind that the omnipotence of the State has always been the prevailing order in West and East.

We need a new approach to the nation state and its relations with global capitalist development mechanisms, in the conviction that the state structure still has a powerful role to play in determining the global capitalist mode of accumulation. Global capitalism exists, even though there is no such thing as a "global" state.

From Hobbes' Leviathan ("that mortal god to which we owe, under the immortal God, our peace and defence") to Hegel's "self-conscious ethical substance", the State is envisaged as a strong, sometimes, despotic element to which rights can be ceded in return for protection. It centralises the monopoly of power within itself to the point of being the supreme end and absolute arbiter of good and evil.

No-one questioned this monolithic situation until the advent of Max Weber. From then on, thinkers began to reflect on forms of power alternative to the "traditional" forms, where authority is not exercised through a specialised administrative apparatus.[40]

Patriarchalism, generally based on a family group, is one example. In this case, power is handed down from one generation to the next through strict hereditary rules. Patrimonialism comes into play when an administrative apparatus develops that is subjugated to the lord by bonds of personal loyalty.

Weber's patrimonialism has enjoyed a resurgence through Eisenstadt[41] and his analysis of modern patrimonial or neo-patrimonial regimes, which are a new slant on traditional regimes and tend to change and expand continuously. At the same time, Juan Linz and Andre Stepan[42] paved the way for the concept of "sultanism" through many comparative studies conducted on authoritarian regimes in Asia, Latin America and Eastern Europe. Such regimes are characterised by the presence of a leader who exercises his power without limitations and with the presence of a family-based or patronal apparatus that derives its power from supporting the leader. Although sultanism may appear to be completely detached from legal and rational rules, it never actually arises in exactly this empirical form. Regimes that resemble these Weberian ideal-types can be found in every part of the world.

We can identify cases approaching standard ideals, including weak authoritarianism, classical traits of the State-Nation relationship, the difficult transition to single party democracy and the role of transnational systems such as the Churches. In a hybrid State, the risk of distortion is high, as we can infer from the constant reference to degenerate phenomena such as nepotism, corruption, conflicts of interest, bending the law to obtain privileges and so on. The State is at the centre of many challenges that undermine its stability and sovereignty, and it is now experiencing an unprecedented crisis of legitimacy referred to as destatisation.

> One example is sub-Saharan Africa where the role of intermediate state powers is expressed more than elsewhere. The concept of State does not exist in various African languages, but is expressed as the power of regulation, justice and peace. Despite their openness to a certain amount of political pluralism, resulting in a form of minimal democracy, the countries of sub-Saharan Africa have to come to terms with resources being in the hands of the old political élites and with the private appropriation of State assets. Communities, their leaders and their symbolic instruments play an

energetic role, often in very original forms, giving rise to the very specific form of governance Africa is currently adopting to penetrate the market economy.[43]

All aspects of Africa (apart from some variants I will identify later) evade categorisation into any of these models because no nations or states have ever succeeded in emerging from its patchwork of historical experiences. Jack Goody,[44] Eisenstadt[45] and Gellner[46] have explored the reason for this in very general terms, but none of the best-known international Africa "experts" have asked themselves this question let alone solved it, which just goes to show how little work has actually been done in this field. The reason is very simple: a nation is born with the advent of written language; spoken language is not enough. This factor is always overlooked but should be remembered particularly on Luther's 500th anniversary. By printing the Bible, Luther created a language that did not previously exist because it had never been printed. Language is the cultural roof of a house that exists but lacks foundations (the State). This process was replicated in Italy, with Dante and Petrarch taking the place of Luther. Many centuries later, Russia found its cultural nationhood in Pushkin's Eugene Onegin. Nothing of this kind happened in Africa, apart from the exceptions I will mention later. It explains why human development in local settlements does not leave ethnicity behind and why ethnicity never develops to the point of establishing itself as a nation, or if it does, it is to destroy and not to rebuild.

One example is the Hutu genocide of the Tutsis. The Rwandan Civil War is a terrifying, yet illuminating, topic for study. The attempted extermination of the Tutsis by the Hutu and the spread of war from Rwanda to Zaire (from April to July 1994, after the first phase of the civil war from October 1990 to August 1993) is enlightening because it reveals that contemporary Rwandan history is perennially marked by an inability to create a state with several nations. Some claim that models of colonisation and then decolonisation are responsible for the failure of African state-building. This suggestion is too black and white: countless episodes can be cited to support neo-colonialism being a dependent or independent variable in this Aristotelian comparison (the part played by French national forces during the extermination of Tutsis by Hutus is an example). The causes of conflict indubitably go back to the Belgian colonisation. This disrupted the existing socioeconomic differentiations—the Hutus were farmers and the Tutsis were herdsmen—where mixed marriages were possible, transforming them into economic and racial differentiations (a quintessentially Eurocentric concept) that led to new socioeconomic differentiations (Tutsis rich, Hutus poor). With decolonisation, the Hutu gained total control of the army and, long before the famous genocide, interracial hatred was sparked that ultimately led to the immense tragedy.[47] Those years marked the start of the tragic wartime migrations that are now a feature of all Africa and have come to affect Europe, because the genocide drove more than a million refugees to Burundi, Zaire, Tanzania and Uganda without any intervention or awareness of the situation by the UN. The US stood in the way of voting on United Nations Security Council Resolution 912 of 1994 condemning the genocide while France stood alongside the Hutu militias throughout the genocide, when they were victorious and later when they were defeated through the intervention of Rwanda and Britain. This affair proves the point that it is impossible to work with generalisations and shows how chaotic this field of study can be.

Another example is the profoundly different role paid by the Portuguese empire in Mozambique and Angola under the pretext of predetermining their post-colonial future: ethnic conflict played an overwhelming part but at the same time the colonisers and colonised intermingled and mixed marriages proliferated. Portugal was ultimately responsible for one of the most substantial cases of state-building in Africa in both Mozambique and Angola. The same is true of its legacy in Brazil. This matter of particular strategic interest is an accepted point but worth repeating. Processes of state-building took place where there was a written language and an imperial historical tradition that was able to withstand colonialism and decolonisation. A language-based route to state-building could be described as Lutheran. In this example, the Bible was replaced by the Koran (which was not translated, like Luther's Bible) and the classic European state was replaced by a tribe that overcame all others by force (the alliance between the Wahhabi sect and the House of Saud) at the end of the eighteenth century, or there was a more clan-like tribal patrilineal succession as practised by the Hashemites of Jordan and particularly the

Alawites of Morocco. The Alawites descend directly from the Prophet and led the process of decolonisation. They make up an extraordinarily strong nation state that is continually reinforcing itself. Egypt is a law unto itself: it existed before Rome and its language was immediately written down, meaning that the multitudes (as we eurocentrically refer to them) have been literate for millennia. Tunisia confirms the theory because, despite all its patrilineal weaknesses, local human settlements still follow the ancient Carthaginian footsteps of Hannibal who challenged Rome by crossing the Alps.

Everything gets more complicated when we leave the lands of Islam to enter the realms of animism, which is the typical cultural context in situations where it is only possible to rise to statehood through old methods of force and extermination. This is an effective method of destruction because it weakens society and builds an absolute or militarised Leviathan of a state with infinite powers of veto but very little ability to construct. This explains why military and religious views must both be considered in order to understand the African question and the weakness of African state-building. One final observation: where there is weak state-building, more than one nation and many patrilineal lines of succession, the classic relationship between nation and internationalisation is quite different, because the vectors of internationalisation have immense penetrating power. The history of Africa is a history of the immense power of internationalisation even in very recent times before and after the Cold War: 20,000 Cubans fighting in Congo (the dark heart of Africa) led by Che Guevara; the Soviets who founded states that survived the fall of the USSR (Tanzania and the Belgian Congo); the Chinese, who export Chinese forced labour to Africa and control most of its infrastructure, as evidenced by the establishment of a military base in Djibouti alongside the existing English, North American, French and Russian bases—and the French with their Central African Franc used in more than ten Central African countries, where they station more than 30,000 soldiers and control all the most important ports.

Of course, South Africa is not Africa, but an Anglo-Boer creation that has recently transformed itself into a new and unknown state identity of Anglican-Soviet origin (as described by Doris Lessing).

References to Africa as a future terrain for the new global economy are numerous and often trivial; it is over-simplistic to say that the demographic boom will give rise to new markets to support development. Although the growing population leads to internal growth and attracts investment, this is often confused, particularly from a Western viewpoint, which is all too often influenced by proto-colonialism.

Africa *is* growing, but in a tumultuous, disorderly and often violent manner. And it is not just growing in size: the growth affects population, economic capacity, infrastructure GDP, yes, but also "politics", or rather policies and governance, meaning models of democracy and governance achieved through an often controversial process of trial and error that is justifiable based on the all-too-recent history of autonomy and independence.

One example is Kenya[48]: this became independent in 1963, when there were nine million unregistered inhabitants. Now there are 45 million inhabitants and the average age is very low. This factor also has a positive effect on the make-up of the ruling class. The country enjoys healthy economic growth of 5% at worst and 8% at best. It has been governed since independence in 1992 by a single party, KANU, heir to the revolutionary movement that brought an end to British colonialism. KANU followed a similar trajectory to the CLN (National Liberation Committee), which controlled Italian resistance after World War II and then came into power.

Since 1992, Kenya has changed its constitution through six difficult electoral cycles with a progressive decrease in tribal conflict, development of an independent judiciary and the rise of various control structures. Much has happened in a few years. Many problems are still unresolved and new ones are cropping up.

For example, the quest for forms of democracy that combine efficiency and representativeness is a process going on in many "Western" countries that are often attracted by "regulated" democracies such as Russia and China; France, governed by Macron and his party, is an example of this attraction. In Kenya, Uhuru Kenyatta consolidated his difficult electoral victory by thinking beyond his second, current mandate to his succession and strengthening the Jubilee Party to take on the mantle of ruling party. For example, the Jubilee Party recently entered into an agreement with the Chinese Communist Party, backing the strong existing economic relations with the Chinese Government and China Development Bank.

State transformation is expected in Africa; the relationship between tribes, regional autonomies, nation states, supranational organisations and businesses is ever-shifting and characterised by grassroots, non-ideological quests for effectiveness and efficiency, apart from some outmoded, differences of opinion.

Kenya has been independent since 1963, which is nothing compared with the history of European and many other countries. The population of Kenyan is made up of 48 tribes divided into a few main ethnic groups. British colonisation left deep roots in military, judicial and administrative aspects of state organisation. Since 1963, government policy has always supported the development and consolidation of a strong national conscience with positive results.

This overlapping of "structures" does not cancel out the sense of belonging: the sense of tribal membership is still strong, especially in socio-familial relationships. This perception is reinforced by the language that each tribe maintains and uses, particularly in "closed" relationships within a limited social group. The sense of belonging affects personal events, from marriages to funerals, but also strengthens business relationships and, all too often, political groupings. Tribal membership is becoming diluted in new generations, but it is still strong and widespread.

Kenyans have a strong feel for their British roots, and the make-up of the diaspora indicates that young people are still strongly attracted to studying and working in Britain.

Kenyans also feel that they are participating in the development of a bright young state, the new Kenya, and they nurture a fair amount of national pride although this is permeated with pragmatism and a quest for efficiency (after all, the state of Kenya is better than the tribes and better than being a colony).

Kenyans also acknowledge the importance of global economic relations by accepting the soft invasion of the China Development Bank, the Gates Foundation and Samsung.

Tribes, states-in-waiting, federative autonomies, historical and cultural ties with colonisers, international roles, participation in the development of global capitalism: it is all happening in Africa and the scenario of change is very interesting.

There is a risk of conformism, potentially sacrificing dynamism and originality in order to adhere to the great communicating networks that are standardising the world in the name of an apparently bearable "iniquity".

Africa is looking to capitalism as a model, convinced that the growth in GDP and investment will lead to a general resurgence, fostering the growth of a strong middle and upper middle class. This is happening to a measurable extent but leaves huge inequalities in its wake that are arguably even more measurable and evident in the unstoppable growth of urban slums. This is part of the fallout of economic transformation, because the cities attract millions of people in a frantic process of internal migration. It is not easy to integrate everyone, and a lack of logistical and reception planning is a particular problem. Social housing is one of the biggest challenges for African governments because it needs strong investment but offers low profitability for greedy international investors.

This situation can be illustrated by snapshots of life in Kenya. Wayaki Way, one of the most important access routes to Nairobi, is thronged with traffic made up of cars, *matutus* (the little white-knuckle minibuses that tear illegally and crazily around the city but are competitive because they pick up thousands of passengers on each round), buses and motorcycles. But the overriding image is of pedestrians: thousands of human beings still walk and run to work, eating up kilometres on foot. Very early in the morning, when the sun is peeping over the horizon, the image of thousands of people streaming along this and other roads towards the city and their jobs is thrilling. The extraordinary image of a hungry crowd invading a city on foot carries a sense of exciting dynamism.

These positive aspects of African dynamism are to some extent being overcome by a copy and paste process leading to loss of originality and disrupting ideas being stamped out in favour of following "Western" models. Even the term "Western" is being washed away by the global spread of standards. The Chinese offer the world models of technological, financial and even social behaviour that are similar to those in the West. These often represent an improvement but cannot be described as disrupting.

Then comes Asia and particularly China. We will see how well the authoritarian balance of Xi Jinping's party state stands up. At present it seems sound and lasting due to its great ability to adapt to global economic dynamics. The things that are fragile in China are democracy and civil society, which are being held to ransom.

In the Antipodes, Pakistan is a "hard" country where the strength of familial bonds in society is inevitably reflected in the political system. The systematic dependency of governments on cronyism weakens the state.

Lastly, in Latin America, the claims of indigenous peoples are combined with local systems of governance. With the acknowledgement of indigenous rights, which have been growing since the 1990s to their present form of twenty-first-century socialism, native populations are helping redesign a new State organisation. Rediscovery of the Federalist model, revised and adapted to these people's need for self-determination, is reviving *metissage* in the form of integration. Neocaciquism and caudillism now represent Latin American people power on a large scale and *terratenientes* or landowners represent it on a local scale.

The starting point for the new perspective advocated by Bertrand Badie[49] involves rejecting a unilinear view of Western modernisation and attempting to find new categories able to accommodate the complex way large public and private organisations operate in contemporary society.

This thinking goes beyond Weber's idea that traditional forms of power could be supplanted by greater institutionalisation. Proponents of the hybrid state include marginal countries but also countries better integrated in global scenarios, seeking their own powers of attraction and thus setting up multifaceted systems of governance to meet today's complex challenges.

Africa, Asia and South America will be state benchmarks for the new century, propelled by modernisation through economic interdependence.[50] Asia is another word for China and India. China is a prime example of full deployment of power and authority, firstly through the authoritarian Asian production system and dynastic empire and secondly under nineteenth-century warlords during the short-lived opium wars. After the communist revolution, power became vested in one of the most ruthless dictatorships of the twentieth century: Asiatic communism. Chinese communism is not the only variant of this: Indochina and North

Korea provide other examples. This power has been brought up to date for the new millennium as a form of monopolistic state capitalism governed by a ruthless oligarchy and technocracy founded on a form of centralised power that is unusual even given the events of the past millennium.

The politics of Chinese state capitalism are based on the rules of restricted citizenship that excludes those who are not wealthy or members of the Communist Party. No other means of access exist. It is impossible to gain access through social and political citizenship because this would be tantamount to liberalism or democracy. Among the models that emerged in the beleaguered twentieth century, the Chinese single party bears no resemblance to the Soviet party torn at the end of World War II by a terrible struggle for survival against foreign capitalist powers and then the Nazis, as well as continuous purges.

Since the revolution, China has never had to fight a war of invasion on its own territory but has shown aggressive tendencies, which have been held at bay by Vietnamese and Soviet communism. Its impressive stability of power remained unaffected even by the Cultural Revolution. The army has always held firmly to the reins of power and has only recently begun negotiations to share some power with the new technocratic class and party members, as evidenced by the recent Chinese Communist Party Congress and to an even greater extent the People's Assembly, set up with the sole intention of ratifying this transition pact. The power transition is bound to be slow and very difficult because it is affected by China's tumultuous, disorderly economic growth, which gives capitalists around the world much to hope for but also much to fear. The rings of power almost overlap: the dictatorship does not allow multiple target communities. Chinese statehood is held firmly together by force alone, brandished as a threat or used within society to stamp out any form of mainstream political dissent. There is no such thing as a citizen.

Keeping up with technological innovation and having to ensure a highly qualified workforce, a Western education in centres of capitalist acculturation involves enormous cost to Chinese society.

Peasants, who make up 50% of the registered workforce (and account for an even greater proportion of the total population), are only allowed to move around within China using a passport: if they evade police control and reach the major cities, this document becomes worthless and they are unidentifiable. Once invisible, not even the very meagre welfare benefits that employment guarantees can alleviate the pains of a labour force subject to a form of exploitation amounting to modern slavery. There are no trade unions or right to strike. Statehood can only be gained through a citizenship of consumption and employment meted out by the ultra-powerful party employment agencies.

Home ownership made possible by selling large state housing complexes and building new neighbourhoods is one way for the new 300–400 million strong middle class to gain access to statehood and civil society. The new moderately wealthy are the most avid supporters of the regime. They will represent the new face of monopolistic state capitalism, together with the peasant bourgeoisie that will arise as soon as pressure by peasants forces the government to convert the fortnightly land rent into a path to ownership. This approach is still highly problematic because it could lead to the rise of a counter-power able to lay the foundations for alternative social power. As opposed to the situation with the "devout" middle classes, loyal to the party that raised them from a state of subjection typical of bureaucratic Confucian domination to a situation where they are sharing wealth with the oligarchs responsible for that domination, this is possible due to a strong resurgence of the age-old cultural heritage of the peasant world.

This path is full of pitfalls and dangers typical of Chinese economic modernisation that I will not dwell on here. China is the eruption of Asiatic despotism in the guise of modern instrumental and managerial rationalism. The resulting political system can only be that of a ruthless neo-capitalist dictatorship with an enormous level of support from the urban middle classes.[51]

Matters in India are very different and more complex. As with the Chinese, the stratification of civilisations has been going on for millennia, combined with a long imperial tradition. India also has a deep-seated tradition of Hindu or Muslim religious faiths while China only observes lay belief systems like Buddhism and Confucianism, although they differ radically from one another. India is a fragment of Europe tossed into Asia because of British rule, which showed its best side in this country. It led to a widespread ruling class and founded a form of statehood governed by law and common law that has withstood the struggle for independence.

The Indian culture of entrepreneurship may be concentrated among Parsi minorities but is still widespread and heterogeneous, and therefore open to international contamination. The Indian diaspora in the world of economics is evidence of this. The Mittal steel group, named after an Indian industrial and service dynasty, confounded financial analysts by launching a successful takeover bid against ARCELOR (created through a merger between companies based in France, Luxembourg and Spain) and becoming the leading global steel colossus. This is common knowledge to anyone who bothers to read the newspapers, not merely a closed circle of experts. India has always been a caste-based society and faces the problem of finding a contemporary way of incorporating the caste system into large-scale capitalist accumulation from an economic and political viewpoint.

History teaches us how India has been able to establish itself as the economic and political power of the new millennium. If we had been able to take a comparative snapshot of the world at the end of the eighteenth century, we would have discovered that economic growth in Asian countries was not so very different from that in Europe. After the eighteenth century, Asia slipped into a decline that has ultimately lasted for two centuries: industrialisation is widespread in Europe and North America and reaching out to conquer the globe from these bases. Everything changed at the beginning of the twentieth century, particularly after World War II, when Asia embarked on a new cycle of economic growth in which industrialisation played an important role, particularly over the last 20 years. Taking a long-term view, development is characterised by emergence from a strong rural civilisation with high population density.

The first nation to emerge was Japan, which has played a role very similar to that of Britain in the nineteenth century, albeit with its own specific characteristics.

Now it is the turn of China and India. Both are emerging as huge markets, torn by bitter conflict between coastal areas and the interior. An extensive sea area stretching from Japan to Indonesia and including coastal China is growing exponentially, particularly around port areas, supported initially by the role of the state and fed by businesses in the diaspora. The impressive turnover of people and commodities in the area has assumed dimensions unprecedented in Europe. Growth in Europe and North America has also been possible due to decisive action by active minorities who have played a leading role on a large scale, but not with the intensity and relevance seen today in India and China.

The path towards industrialisation will come about, as was the case in Europe, through urbanisation, or (as many states in the area seem to desire) the overall transformation of productive activities and services may be limited by a wish to maintain a stable rural population. As things stand at present, it is different to answer the one crucial question: will decentralised industry dominate in India, or will it follow a European model? Although India has completely reinvented itself, it remains a peasant nation with clear social and territorial inequalities, determined by a federal state structure and the immensity of the continent. The creation of a broad strata of middle classes and bourgeoisie with a strong tendency towards service innovation, now an acknowledged fact, will be crucial to India's development. These entities are linked to international trade and unequal exchange with the metropolises of capitalist accumulation and also have deep indigenous roots in individual Indian states.

We believe that political growth in India will follow a different pattern to European growth because aspects such as ethnicity and religious affiliation are very important in the Indian continent and are organised as systems of communication and interrelationship between the élites and the people. The value system is expressed not only by religion but also by the formidable construct that is the Asian family system, which permeates economic relations and structures in a very special way. However, it is unclear how this tradition affects the orientation of the Asian middle classes, who are now affected by typically North American and European models of economic and social organisation that they must deploy in a very different cultural and social context.

Non-Asian agents of economic globalisation are applying pressure for markets to expand into India without external diseconomies of corruption, cronyism and nepotism. These factors will be revealed as India changes from an economy based on primary sectors and goods to a more complex and interdependent economy. At this point, a series of factors that once seemed to pave the way for growth now impede growth.

Human rights claims are crucial to constructing a state of law. Without this, the contracts crucial to building an Indian market and political system cannot be fully reliable.

India is a great democracy with powerful trade unions and huge mass political parties with local roots that underwent an overwhelming transformation after the birth of the Hindu Nationalist Party. This party played a very positive role at social level: much of the upward mobilisation and political inclusion of the untouchable caste was party-based, forcing the historic party of the Gandhi dynasty, the Congress Party, to change radically from a party of Oxford-educated Brahmins to a party intent on gathering a consensus extending beyond the middle classes and urban workers to the rural world. The party is also strengthening its historic ties with some trade union and collateral organisations that supported Nehru and his daughter Indira in the past.

India also injects an unusual dose of violence into its political struggles, as the tragic history of this dynasty shows. The tragedy of life lies in reincarnation and in the succession of seasons of body and mind. The religious and ethnic division is bound to explode, at times, of the greatest crises. The state must seek to establish itself as an instrument for regulating conflict and neutralising violence, even though civil society has not yet consolidated itself into a political society open to debate but is still a society of conflict, dominated by an approach based on friendship and enmity.

This phenomenon re-poses the conundrum of whether civil society is a force for institutionalising economic and non-economic relations in India. If it is, this is not happening under the same terms as in Europe. In India, the role of the political and economic power élites is crucial, and the part played by group associations and pluralism is very strong, as in the English-speaking and European intellectual and political tradition. Yet the political parties are also very strong, and this is an exceptional situation in Asia's history. The polyarchy is showing a different face with regard to de facto situational power. Similarly, the relation between state and market is very different from the one that has grown up in Europe and North America. It is not organised as a dialectic of opposites but as an interplay of compromises, mediations and continual adjustments, even though the push towards liberalisation and the opening up of relations with international markets continually recategorises and reshapes the role of the state.

In any case, the shape of the relationship between the state, market and companies is very uneven within the Asian continent, as we have seen.

One sign of this unevenness is the extraordinary variety of employment issues within the Asian continent, including India, Indonesia, Taiwan and Japan. The social stratification of classes and strata intersect with ethnic dimensions, sexual division, dependence on external European and North American models and resistance to these due to workers' cultural roots and social relationships. Concepts such as "collective movements", "trade union organisation", "social conflict" and so on take on completely different connotations in Asia to those in Europe and North America.

The striking thing in India is the deep-seated resemblance of the Indian party system to the European party system. In the geography of political science and party machinery, India is to Europe as Europe is to Chile. This Latin American nation bordering the Pacific Ocean has come up with an impressive simulacrum of European political structures, without deep-rooted populism and without the fragmentation of political parties typical of most of South America. We need only think of the formation of Indian Communist Parties and the governing roles they play in important states, despite divisions imposed by Chinese pressure, which are nevertheless neutralised by national conflict. This unusual situation makes India different from the rest of Asia.

The Indonesian coup of 1964 paved the way for modern Asian dictatorships coloured by a capitalist, post-feudal modernisation. This coup meant the massacre of millions of communists and followers of the national state founder in the struggle against the Dutch: General Sukarno. His successor, the dictator Suharno, who still basks in echoes of approval from the international press and enjoys significant prestige among the country's ruling classes, marked a turning point in the history of Asia as a whole, not merely the south-east. India is also part of this story.

When we think that during the same span of years, the Communist parties were stamped out in Sudan and the Middle East, we realise that India is a democratic enclave in the tormented political history of Asia where violence is the only option in the absence of polyarchy as a set of electoral (i.e. democratically elected) processes and de facto situational powers.

Whatever India's future, its exceptional status is irreversible and will remain an indelible factor in the global history of political participation and institutionalisation.[52]

The scenario in South America is very different, because the community of destiny broke up after the shattering of Simon Bolivar's dream of creating one South American state uniting the two oceans in order to challenge Europe and North America on equal terms. Instead, the result was a myriad of nationless states because in South America, unlike Europe and the US, the state always goes before the nation. This is due to specific policies on inclusion and the consolidation of aggressive pressures still present in the continental states. When the Spanish colonial empire broke up, it left a host of states torn apart by a long and complex consolidation process that set the coastal trading oligarchies and the farmers of the interior against one another, with the additional problem of extensive infighting and widespread violence. In 1949 in Colombia, a civil war between the Blanco Party and the Colorado Party led to 40,000 deaths and fighting on a large scale, following decisions by social and interest groups that began to sink their roots during the early days of anti-Spanish decolonisation.

Ultimately, much less blood was shed by the armies of Cortez, when they exterminated or reduced the native peoples to a state of impotence, than that shed on South America's campuses and valleys during wars between people who not long before had been fighting shoulder to shoulder against Spanish rule.

The history of Brazil, part of the old Portuguese colonial empire, is completely different. Even though the country is vast, the colonial state did not implode. Why? Firstly, because the Portuguese monarchy still has a firm grip on the reins in Brazil. After being thrown out of Portugal by the Napoleonic armies, the family did not return even after Waterloo, due to the Constitution of Cadiz desired by republican constitutionalists and a difficult diplomatic situation. The Brazilian Empire was to continue almost until the turn of the twentieth century. Its echoes lived on in the role still played in Republican Brazil by a bureaucratic and technocratic class educated for centuries, at least up to the time of Napoleon, in the Portuguese metropolis, within and without the cloistered walls of the University of Coimbra—not back home in the South American viceroys, as was the case for representatives of the Spanish Empire. This background allowed Brazil to build a cohesive and strongly centralised state structure despite its federalism.

Sovereignty is a serious matter and cannot be threatened by the blows of one regional oligarchy against another.

Despite its strong statehood, Brazil has never formed national parties throughout its history. The Bolivarian centralist obsession was played out at Central State level, but the federal form of the state froze the ruling classes of each region into a local party system with consequent fragmentation of the national party. Only two political phenomena succeeded in breaking up this state of affairs. The first, which occurred between the two world wars, was the developmentalist populism of Getúlio Vargas, with its emphasis on growth and the fight against inequality that paralysed local oligarchies and mobilised the impoverished masses, the landless and workers in the big cities in support of "Caesarist" movements. Vargism lingered on as a variant of South American populism and has left an irreversible mark on Brazilian history.

The second phenomenon was the Workers' Party set up by Lula, who was president of Brazil and had a long history as a trade unionist. In this case too, the roots lie in an anti-oligarchic mobilisation of the masses through a totalitarian choice between belonging to the party and belonging to the union. This is typical of classic populism and in my opinion differentiates it from other movements that masquerade under the same name but are actually Caesarist, Bonapartist and so on. The phenomenon is very different in the case of President Lula's party. In this case, we are dealing with a modern trade union that grew up with the help of the AFL CIO and the Italian CISL against patronage and savage injustices meted out in Brazilian factories. It also had to withstand penetration by Castro and the presence of Marxist and Trotskyist undercurrents that are still at work in the party and trade unions within the working-class belt of San Paolo.

Brazil's cultural and political hegemony has now firmly returned to the hands of an oligarchic economic leadership group closely linked to liberal financial capital. This "vendedora" bourgeoisie will encounter heavy contradictions in the political cycle: no party has ever had the majority in Parliament, and every government throughout Brazil's history has always been forced to a hasty process of cut and thrust with allies in a situation affected by unusual fragmentation of local representation. This situation lies at the heart of all political corruption afflicting Brazil.

This has led to the ongoing instability of the polyarchy: the de facto situational economic power is very divided and very locally fragmented and seeks the support of different party groupings as and when needed. This can take place on a local or national scale. Everything depends on how economics meets politics: at federal or central level. This results in the coexistence of very different political landscapes. This situation may represent the future of Brazilian and even South American polyarchy as the neo-liberal cycle emerging throughout the continent gathers pace, just as it is declining in Europe. The legal unity of the Brazilian state is falling apart under the impact of globalisation and the bewitching power of economic liberalism, which can be seen as beneficial or evil depending on which faction you belong to. On the other hand, growing local political fragmentation will always prevent sovereignty from becoming established.

Brazil has therefore seen a rapid decline in the great social progress achieved during the political reign of Lula's Workers' Party and the economic reign of the big state oil companies and the big "reformist" industrial monopolies, opposed by service and telecommunications groups and all the small and medium-sized agricultural property owners disgruntled by Workers' Party reforms.

The nation is again being torn apart by poverty, crime, unemployment and drug cartels that have resumed their usual murderous business.

This country of 147 million voters has emerged from 13 consecutive years of left-wing government under the Workers' Party, leading to the presidency of Lula and then Dilma Rousseff (and the centrist Temer, after Rousseff's impeachment). After the economic miracle came the great crisis following the Lava Jato (Operation Car Wash) scandal. In 2018, we saw the rise to power of Jair Bolsonaro, a former Army captain and social media phenomenon (he has over seven million followers on Facebook alone), achieved through nostalgia for the old military dictatorship interspersed with openly homophobic and misogynistic views. Bolsonaro is the new Brazilian president and cannot be compared to any other right-wing world leader: he is not the new face of politics and his election is unpopular with the markets because he is ushering in a policy of neo-liberalism and privatisations.[53]

The situation in Brazil is the best argument for Kalecki's *intermediate regimes*,[54] but also fuels the claims of its critics who discern its weakness, suggesting that the collapse of the USSR led to the resurgence of the form of oligarchic, financialised capitalism that transformed the country at the end of the twentieth century.

This process was punctuated by the historical specificities of economic and social structures typical of global capitalism, constantly subject to the law of unequal development. Leon Trotsky's seminal works[55] on this subject that are essential for understanding the universal and transcendent implications of political struggle are no longer read.

Our future is held in a balance between an Asian dictatorship based on monopolistic state capitalism, the European foothold in Asia, South American fragmentation and the emergence of Africa. The writing is on the wall, but we are closing our eyes and hoping it will go away.

Notes

1. N. D. Kondratiev, "*Die langen* Sozialwissenschaft und Sozialpolitik" 56: 573–609, 1926, returned to in Review of Economic Statistics (1935) and again in "*The Long Waves in Economic Life.*" Review of Economic Statistics 17 (6): 105–115. 1935. After his death, shot during the purges of 1938, his main works were collected in *Dynamics of Economic Development: Long Cycles and Industrial Growth in Historical Context.* London: Macmillan, 1998.
2. W. Eucken, *Die Grundlagen der Nationalökonomie.* Fischer, Jena, 1940.
3. M. Kalecki, *Political Aspects of Full Employment*, Political Quarterly, 1943, n. 14, pp. 322–331.
4. Investments in nationalised branches can help solve the problem of unemployment only if they are made using criteria different from those adopted by private enterprise. Public enterprises must be prepared to settle for a lower rate of profit and plan their investments in order to cushion economic crises. (In text).

5. One essential reference to this topic can be found in the long series of reflections by B. Amoroso, *Europa e Mediterraneo. Le sfide del futuro* Editore Dedalo, Bari 2000, *with* J. Jespersen, *Un' Europa possibile. Dalla crisi alla cooperazione Publisher* Castelvecchi, Siena, 2015, *Figli di troika. Gli artefici della crisi economica* Publisher Castelvecchi, Siena, 2013.
6. J. Rueff, *Défense et illustration de l'étalon-or*, Paris, Alcan, 1932.
7. K. Mannheim, *Das Problem der Generationen*, in "Kölner Vierteljahres Hefte für Soziologie", 1928, VII, pp. 157–185, 309–330.
8. G. Sapelli, *Southern Europe since 1945, Portugal, Spain, Italy, Greece and Turkey, Tradition and Modernity*, Longam, London–New York–New Delhi, 1994.
9. D. P. Calleo *Follies of Power: America's Unipolar Fantasy*, Cambridge University Press, Cambridge, 2009.
10. On the subject, see F. Caudullo and G. Sapelli, *La dottrina Obama e le sue conseguenze*, published by goWare, Florence, 2015.
11. F. Chabod, *Carlo V e il suo impero*, Einaudi, Torino, 1985.
12. On this subject, see my book *Un nuovo mondo. La rivoluzione di Trump e i suoi effetti globali*, Guerini & Associati, Milan, 2017.
13. B, Jessop, *The State. Past. Present. Future*, Polity Press, Cambridge, 2016.
14. G. Sapelli, *Chi comanda in Italia*, Guerini e Associati, 2013.
15. G. Sapelli, *Southern Europe, cit.*
16. G. Sapelli, *op. cit.*
17. W. Eucken, *op. cit.*
18. W. Röpke, *International Order and Economic Integration*, Springer, Heidelberg–London, 1959.
19. H. Minsky, *The Financial Instability Hypothesis.* In "Jerome Levy Economics Institute", Working Paper No. 74. 1992.
20. F. Bozo, *Histoire secrète de la crise irakienne*, Perrin, Paris, 2013.
21. D. P. Calleo, *The German Problem Reconsidered: Germany and the World Order 1870 to the Present*, Cambridge University Press, Cambridge, 1978.
22. A. Naaman, *Les Alawites*, Erick Bonnier, Paris, 1999.
23. M. Kessler, *La politique étrangère de la France*, Presse de Sciences Po, 1999.
24. Wallerstein, I., *The rise and the future demise of the world capitalist system: concepts and comparative analysis*, in "Comparative studies in society and history", 1974, XVI, pp. 387–415.

    Wallerstein, I., *The capitalist world economy*, Cambridge, 1979.

Wallerstein, I., *The modern world-system II. Mercantilism and the consolidation of the European world-economy, 1600–1750*, New York, 1980.

25. S. Amin, *Les défis de la mondialisation*, 1996.

    Pensée sociale critique pour le XXIe *siècle: mélanges en l'honneur de Saint-Amin*, Éditions L'Harmattan, Paris, 2003.

    S. Amin, The Liberal Virus: Permanent War and the Americanization of the World, 2004, *le Virus libéral*, version française, Paris, le Temps des cerises.

    S. Amin, Ali El Kenz, *Europe and the Arab world; patterns and prospects for the new relationship*, 2005.

    S. AminL'Éveil du Sud, le Temps des cerises, Paris, 2008.

    S. Amin, Du capitalisme à la civilisation, Éditions Syllepse, Lyon, 2008.

26. L. Pasinetti, *Growth and Income Distribution – Essays in Economic Theory*, Cambridge: Cambridge University Press, 1974.

27. P. M. Sweezy, *The Theory of Capitalist Development*, Oxford University Press, 1942.

    P. A. Baran, P. M. Sweezy, *Monopoly Capital. An Essay on the American Economic and Social Order*, Monthly Review Press, 1966.

    P. M. Sweezy, *Modern Capitalism and other essays, Monthly Review Press*, 1972.

28. M. Godelier, (edité par), *Transitions et subordinations au capitalisme, Editions de la Maison des Sciences de l' Homme, Paris, 1984.*

29. Edited by J. Osiatyński, Collected Works of Michal Kalecki. Volume V: Developing Economies, Clarendon Press Publication, Oxford, 1993 and particularly *Intermediate regimes*, published in M. Kalecki, *The Last Phase in the Transformation of Capitalism* (With an Introduction of G.R. Feiwel), Monthly Review Press, New York, 1972, pp. 115–124.

30. M. McCartney and B. Harriss-White, *The 'Intermediate Regime' and 'Intermediate Classes' Revisited: A Critical Political Economy of Indian Economic Development from 1980 to Hindutva, QEH Working Paper Series – QEHWPS34* Working Paper Number 34, pp. 14–18.

31. B. Badie, *Quand le Sud reinvent le monde. Essai sur la puissabnce de la faiblesse*, La Decouvert, Paris, 2018, p. 16.

32. R. Luxemburg, *Die Akkumulation des Kapitals. Ein Beitrag zur ökonomischen Erklärung des Imperialismus*. Vorwärts, Berlin, 1913.

33. See, M. Turchetto, *Leggere L'accumulazione del capitale*, in "Rivista telematica di studi sulla memoria femminile", n. 28, 2015.

34. D. Pilling, *China's entry into Africa comes with a warning*, in "Financial Times", 27 September 2018, p. 13.
35. J. Needham *The Genius of China* (A one-volume distillation by R. Temple), Simon & Schuster, New York, 1986.
36. J. Gernet, *Le Monde chinois: 3. L'époque contemporaine. xxe siècle*, Paris, Armand Colin, 2005 (1re éd., 1972)).
37. K. A. Wittfogel, *Oriental Despotism. A comparative study of total power.* Yale University Press, New Haven, 1957.
38. A. T. Mahan *The Influence of Sea Power Upon History, 1660–1805*, New Haven, Abridged, 1980.
39. G. Sapelli, *Da Mao a Xi Jinping, note sul XIX congresso del PCC* (a cura di N. Bianconi) in "Cina. La voce del potere", GoWare Edizioni, Firenze, 2018, pp. 7–24.
40. M. Weber, *Die drei reinen Typen der legitimen Herrschaft*, in "*Preußische Jahrbücher*". 187, 1922, S. 1–12, pp. 475–488.
41. S. Eisenstadt, *European Civilization in a Comparative Perspective, Cambridge University Press, Cambridge, 1972.*
42. J. Linz and A. Stepan, *Modern Nondemocratic Regimes* in *Problems of Democratic Transition & Consolidation*, Johns Hopkins University Press, Baltimore, 1996.
43. V. Ronchi, *Lo stato ibrido*, Introduction to the issue of Equilibri 2/2018, 199–201.
44. J. Goody, *Production and Reproduction***,** Cambridge University Press, 1977.
45. S. Eisenstadt, *op. cit.*
46. E. Gellner, *Nations and Nationalism*, Cornell University Press, Ithaca, 2008.
47. G. Prunier, *Africa's World War: Congo, the Rwandan Genocide, and the Making of Continental Catastrophe*, Oxford University Press, 2009.
48. M. Citelli, Il Kenya: laboratorio africano, Equilibri 2/2018, 276–282.
49. B. badie, *op. cit.*
50. The following discussion is based on my book G. Sapelli, *Global Challenges and the Emerging World Order*, Singer, 2015.
51. This analysis is again based on B. Moore Jr, *Social Origins of Dictatorship and Democracy. Lord and Peasant in the Making of the Modern World*, Beacon Press, Boston, 1966.
52. S. K. Majumdar, *Lost Glory: India's Capitalism Story*, Oxford, Oxford University Press, 2017.

53. J. Souza, *A elite do atraso: Da escravidão à Lava Jato*. Rio de Janeiro: Leya. 2017.
54. M. Kaleckh, *op. cit.*
55. See the still-unsurpassed essay by M. C. Howard and J. E. King, *A History of Marxian Economics, 1929–1990*, Macmillan International Higher Education, London, 1992, pp. 222–242.

Bibliography

N. D. Kondratiev, "*Die langen* Sozialwissenschaft und Sozialpolitik" 56: 573–609, 1926, returned to in Review of Economic Statistics (1935) and again in "*The Long Waves in Economic Life*." Review of Economic Statistics 17 (6): 105–115. 1935. After his death, shot during the purges of 1938, his main works were collected in *Dynamics of Economic Development: Long Cycles and Industrial Growth in Historical Context*. London: Macmillan, 1998.

W. Eucken, *Die Grundlagen der Nationalökonomie*. Fischer, Jena, 1940a.

M. Kalecki, *Political Aspects of Full Employment*, Political Quarterly, 1943, n. 14, pp. 322–331.

B. Amoroso, *Europa e Mediterraneo. Le sfide del futuro* Editore Dedalo, Bari 2000, with J. Jespersen, *Un'Europa possibile. Dalla crisi alla cooperazione*. Publisher Castelvecchi, Siena, 2015, *Figli di troika. Gli artefici della crisi economica* Publisher Castelvecchi, Siena, 2013.

J. Rueff, *Défense et illustration de l'étalon-or*, Paris, Alcan, 1932.

K. Mannheim, *Das Problem der Generationen*, in "Kölner Vierteljahres Hefte für Soziologie", 1928, VII, pp. 157–185, 309–330.

G. Sapelli, *Southern Europe since 1945, Portugal, Spain, Italy, Greece and Turkey, Tradition and Modernity*, Longam, London–New York–New Delhi, 1994.

D. P. Calleo *Follies of Power: America's Unipolar Fantasy*, Cambridge University Press, Cambridge, 2009.

F. Caudullo and G. Sapelli, *La dottrina Obama e le sue conseguenze*, published by goWare, Florence, 2015.

F. Chabod, *Carlo V e il suo impero*, Einaudi, Torino, 1985.

G. Sapelli, *Un nuovo mondo. La rivoluzione di Trump e i suoi effetti globali*, Guerini & Associati, Milan 2017.

B. Jessop, *The State. Past. Present. Future*, Polity Press, Cambridge, 2016.

G. Sapelli, *Chi comanda in Italia*, Guerini e Associati, 2013.

W. Eucken, *Die Grundlagen der Nationalökonomie*. Fischer, Jena, 1940b.

W. Röpke, *International Order and Economic Integration*, Springer, Heidelberg–London, 1959.
H. Minsky, *The Financial Instability Hypothesis*. In "Jerome Levy Economics Institute," Working Paper No. 74. 1992.
F. Bozo, Histoire secrète de la crise irakienne, Perrin, Paris, 2013.
D. P. Calleo, The German Problem Reconsidered: Germany and the World Order 1870 to the Present, Cambridge University Press, Cambridge, 1978.
A. Naaman, *Les Alawites*, Erick Bonnier, Paris, 1999.
M. Kessler, *La politique étrangère de la France*, Presse de Sciences Po, 1999.
I. Wallerstein, The rise and the future demise of the world capitalist system: concepts and comparative analysis, in "Comparative studies in society and history", 1974, XVI, pp. 387–415.
I. Wallerstein, The capitalist world economy, Cambridge, 1979.
I. Wallerstein, The modern world-system II. Mercantilism and the consolidation of the European world-economy, 1600–1750, New York, 1980.
S. Amin, Les défis de la mondialisation, 1996.
Pensée sociale critique pour le XXIe siècle: mélanges en l'honneur de Saint-Amin, Éditions L'Harmattan, Paris, 2003.
S. Amin, Ali El Kenz, Europe and the Arab world; patterns and prospects for the new relationship, 2005.
S. Amin, L'Éveil du Sud, le Temps des cerises, Paris, 2008.
S. Amin, Du capitalisme à la civilisation, Éditions Syllepse, Lyon, 2008.
L. Pasinetti, Growth and Income Distribution – Essays in Economic Theory, Cambridge: Cambridge University Press, 1974.
P. M. Sweezy, The Theory of Capitalist Development, Oxford University Press, 1942.
P. A. Baran, P. M. Sweezy, Monopoly Capital. An Essay on the American Economic and Social Order, Monthly Review Press, 1966.
P. M. Sweezy, Modern Capitalism and other essays, Monthly Review Press, 1972.
M. Godelier, (edité par), Transitions et subordinations au capitalisme, Editions de la Maison des Sciences de l' Homme, Paris, 1984.
Edited by J. Osiatyński, Collected Works of Michal Kalecki. Volume V: Developing Economies, Clarendon Press Publication, Oxford, 1993 and particularly Intermediate regimes, published in M. Kalecki, The Last Phase in the Transformation of Capitalism (With an Introduction of G. R. Feiwel), Monthly Review Press, New York, 1972, pp. 115–124.
M. McCartney and B. Harriss-White, The 'Intermediate Regime' and 'Intermediate Classes' Revisited: A Critical Political Economy of Indian

Economic Development from 1980 to Hindutva, QEH Working Paper Series - QEHWPS34 Working Paper Number 34, pp. 14–18.
B. Badie, Quand le Sud reinvent le monde. Essai sur la puissabnce de la faiblesse, La Decouvert, Paris, 2018a, p. 16.
R. Luxemburg, Die Akkumulation des Kapitals. Ein Beitrag zur ökonomischen Erklärung des Imperialismus. Vorwärts, Berlin, 1913.
M. Turchetto, Leggere L'accumulazione del capitale, in "Rivista telematica di studi sulla memoria femminile", n. 28, 2015.
D. Pilling, China's entry into Africa comes with a warning, in "Financial Times", 27 September 2018, p. 13.
J. Needham, The Genius of China. (A one-volume distillation by R. Temple), Simon & Schuster, New York, 1986.
J. Gernet, *Le Monde chinois: 3. L'époque contemporaine. xxe siècle*, Paris, Armand Colin, 2005 (1re éd., 1972).
K. A. Wittfogel, Oriental Despotism. A comparative study of total power. Yale University Press, New Haven, 1957.
T. Mahan, The Influence of Sea Power Upon History, 1660–1805, New Haven, Abridged, 1980.
G. Sapelli, Da Mao a Xi Jinping, note sul XIX congresso del PCC (a cura di N. Bianconi) in "Cina. La voce del potere", GoWare Edizioni, Firenze, 2018, pp. 7–24.
M. Weber, *Die drei reinen Typen der legitimen Herrschaft,* in "*Preußische Jahrbücher*". 187, 1922, S. 1–12, pp. 475–488.
S. Eisenstadt, *European Civilization in a Comparative Perspective,* Cambridge University Press, Cambridge, 1972.
J. Linz and A. Stepan, *Modern Nondemocratic Regimes* in *Problems of Democratic Transition & Consolidation*, Johns Hopkins University Press, Baltimore, 1996.
V. Ronchi, *Lo stato ibrido*, Introduction to the issue of Equilibri 2/2018, 199–201.
J. Goody, Production and Reproduction, Cambridge University Press, 1977.
E. Gellner, *Nations and Nationalism*, Cornell University Press, Ithaca, 2008.
G. Prunier, *Africa's World War: Congo, the Rwandan Genocide, and the Making of Continental Catastrophe*, Oxford University Press, 2009.
M. Citelli, Il Kenya: laboratorio africano, Equilibri 2/2018, 276–282.
B. Badie, *Quand le Sud reinvent le monde. Essai sur la puissabnce de la faiblesse*, La Decouvert, Paris, 2018b, p. 16.
G. Sapelli, *Global Challenges and the Emerging World Order*, Springer, 2015.
B. Moore Jr, *Social Origins of Dictatorship and Democracy. Lord and Peasant in the Making of the Modern World*, Beacon Press, Boston, 1966.

S. K. Majumdar, *Lost Glory: India's Capitalism Story*, Oxford, Oxford University Press, 2017.
J. Souza, *A elite do atraso: Da escravidão à Lava Jato*. Rio de Janeiro: Leya. 2017.
M. Kaleckh, *op. cit.*
M. C. Howard and J. E. King *A History of Marxian Economics, 1929–1990*, Macmillan International Higher Education, London, 1992, pp. 222–242.

2

Financialised, High-tech Capitalism Based on Modern Slavery

The Advent of Owner Capitalism: Ordoliberalism and New Technologies

There is a widespread, almost sickening belief that a new socioeconomic order (albeit still capitalist) is emerging from the global economic crisis.

This is nothing new: the vicissitudes of productive forces are always intimately linked with forms of production and thus social relations. In the history of capitalist deployment, social relations, which have very little to do with mechanics and determinism, have always played a crucial role in shaping productive forces.

Labour is the most sensitive and relevant seismograph for indicating changes in relationships between forms of accumulation and social relationships of production.

In this instance, I mean living labour, embedded in the network of contractual relations wrapped around the workforce: the part of working time shaped by the capitalist relationship. The thing that is sold or commissioned is not, heaven forfend, all the work performed by the

G. Sapelli, *Beyond Capitalism*, https://doi.org/10.1007/978-3-030-20769-4_2

working person, as in relationships of slavery, but only work performed during the time the person is subject to social employment relations.

Nowadays, however, the time during which the person is subject to these relations is in the hands of capitalists alone and they can bring to bear a formidable legal system that puts all the cards in their hands ("liberalisation of the labour market") and the constant threat of using force in a context of high unemployment and very low-cost labour force reproducibility, which has led to the advent of a new social form of production.

It amounts to financialised capitalism and has all the hallmarks of modern slavery, which still remains to be properly analysed.

Modern slavery differs from ancient forms of slavery because it lacks the factor responsible for perpetuating slavery: management of reproduction, which was previously in the hands of the slave master responsible for managing the family of slaves.

These days we are left with the worst part of slavery, which is absolute de facto discretionality over all working times and workloads (from the most physical to the most qualified), leaving the workforce responsible for its own reproduction.

In a system of deflation, low wages and continuously precarious employment with a very serious demographic knock-on effect and steadily declining profit margin (inevitable given these social production ratios), a new historical and social construct is taking shape: financial capitalism based on modern slavery.

To understand what has changed in recent decades, we must go back beyond the current crisis to its origins.

These include a range of linked effects that are only apparently distinct from one another.

One dates back to the collapse of the Bretton Woods system between 1971 and 1973, when the dollar ceased to be a benchmark currency and the world ventured into a system of high interest rates and very volatile relations between currencies. Surplus liquidity created by a stepping-up of oligopolistic relations in the world trade in raw materials led to a deep-seated shift between the value of production and the resulting extra work and the value of circulating currency.

This began to generate much stronger rates of growth in value than in the past, in a self-perpetuating cycle.

The money-commodity-money cycle, where there was always more money at the end than at the beginning due to surplus value achieved during production, was joined by a new factor. Money became a commodity in its own right, through a radical transformation in exchange mechanisms and rules (derivatives et al., exchanged in shadow banks and shadow pools) to create further masses of money that could in turn gain value.[1]

At the same time, managerial capitalism, where ownership was separate from control and the manager ruled the shareholders, was gradually replaced by owner capitalism, where the shareholders nominally rule over the manager while actually the opposite is true, as demonstrated by the stock options and spiralling salaries of top managers.

While ostensibly celebrating shareholder value, we are actually paving the way for the predominance of fat-cat managers, who are paid in accordance with algorithms that are a mystery to shareholders and capitalists alike.

The only way this can be linked to labour is the manner in which productive forces develop.

The start of this intersection between owner capitalism, ruled over by stock option-holding managers and the development of productive forces came to a head in the long uninterrupted growth cycle of the US economy, lasting from the late 1980s to the first half of the noughties.

This long cycle, when it seemed that capitalism could do no wrong, was underpinned by the intersection of capitalism with the ICT, that is, with the new Kondatrieff[2] cycle of telecommunication innovation clusters, development of electromagnetism for space travel and the miniaturisation capabilities of rare earths.

Labour productivity grew dramatically. This was due to two factors: lowering of transaction costs as time and space costs tended to zero and the development of growing shares of surplus value to coincide with the creation of huge masses of domestic demand.

Demand seemed to become the essential factor in markets where this process began, first and foremost in the English-speaking world subject to common law, but also to a lesser extent in continental Europe, subject to Roman and Germanic law.

Markets had to be created in what were once called developing countries and are now referred to as BRICS. Of course, as we all know today, markets that generated the illusion that all the supposedly advanced economies could be founded on export-led models did not develop as expected.

Aggregate demand followed the huge shift of income from labour to capital, resulting in a collapse in domestic demand and the coming into being of an export-led model with deflation and the collapse of consumption and wages.

Now we are wallowing in a deep global aggregate demand crisis due to the effect of the long-term deflationary policy triggered by German *ordoliberismus* and global austerity policies guided by an oligarchy based on mixed (i.e. political and technical) technocracy and German ideological domination of the European Union without national monetary sovereignty.

Thus began (initially invisibly, then institutionally) a gigantic crisis of productive overcapacity that continually threatens capitalist reproduction and that of society.

This is particularly reflected by a colossal reduction in the workforce employed worldwide as well as enormous stockpiles of unsold goods. It is hardly surprising that the average size of companies on a global scale has been falling for about 30 years due to the intensification of high-tech productivity, all in the name of labour saving.

We must not let ourselves be deceived by the creation of the new Asian proletariat, which is now an established fact and involves hundreds of millions of new proletarians.

This is a temporary phenomenon: it will not last more than 50 years, which is the bat of an eyelid in historical terms, because the new proletariat will very soon feel the impact (it already has) of Gerschenkron's[3] law of the advantage of backwardness, that is the fact that not all stages of technological growth take place in India, China, Malaysia, Burma, Singapore, Peru and so on. Instead, these stages are skipped, and we cling to the last available stage for the production of surplus value—hence the dwindling workforce.

There are still immense pockets of relative surplus value, but these are created by long working days and low wages rather than by technology.

This phenomenon always goes hand in hand with capitalist accumulation and, as I will argue later, has now made its reappearance. This explodes any technological determinism right here in the old continent, under the heel of German ordoliberalism. This system responds to a drop in the profit margin by lowering wages and deflation, thus perpetually generating new meltdowns triggered by under-consumption, like those currently under way in Europe.

What role does finance play in this interesting analytical scenario associated with great social misery?

It is no longer a variant of the classic production of surplus value through the acquisition of surplus labour due to commanded labour described by Ricardo.

It has become something more, that is a tool masking a falling trend in the rate of profit generated by rising unemployment, hence by the collapse of living labour and also by the growing overproduction crisis causing the non-solvency of demand.

Finance is used to play for time, because the above process has turned any company able to generate significant amounts of cash flow into a new type of company creating a value generated by financialisation, alongside the value generated by production. This is done by extending the circulation of money against money and particularly by managing indebtedness to the point of selling debt against debt, with very high rates of risk and return.

This process has invested in non-bank-centred systems such as those available in the English-speaking world, as well as European bank-centred systems, all institutions whose purpose is not to disburse funds but to create monetary value from money, such as investment funds and the like.[4]

We only became aware of this in 2007, with the crisis sparked by excess risk that led to the collapse of Lehman Brothers.

All global states had a hand in this process, supported it through Clinton and Blair-style deregulation, spreading a sense of security that the state would intervene to save what could be saved just as happened during the great crisis in US savings banks in the late 1980s.

This was not the case in 2007. The temporary non-rescue carried out was dictated more by fear and technical inexperience than anything else.

As we all now know, the next step is for the state to intervene by nationalising the banks or financing industries using high-risk loans (Obama and the US automobile industry is an example). We need only look at the growing role of central banks with New York-style policies to shore up social disintegration.[5]

Because the state has always intervened, we can really talk about the global rise in a new form of monopolistic state capitalism that seeks to address the industrial crisis and resulting unemployment as well as excess risk through its interventions.

The rise of this new financially dominated monopolistic state capitalism is opposed by German and Nordic ordoliberalism, backed by a long intellectual tradition, which profoundly changed the balance of power in Europe through the unification of Germany in the 1990s.

Ordoliberalism has all the characteristics of financialised capitalism as described above but differs in that the system of free competition has effectively replaced the power system: it imposes lower wages, lower public spending and the destruction of welfare in all other European states that are unable to pursue its export-led model with the same assiduousness. At the same time, it ensures multiple ways of allocating property right and allows the state to play the internal role of stepping in to replace the principle of subsidiarity when this fails yet bans all other European states from doing the same.[6]

It does this by controlling European institutions without public legitimacy, with impressive firmness and continuity, as evidenced by ongoing European deflation.

However, the mechanism for consolidating finance in production has been fully reversed even in Europe and the effects on labour are therefore very similar to those previously described at global level. These include mass unemployment due to a restricted productive base, lowering of income due to a reduction in the wage bill, a meltdown in small production units that are unable to generate the financialisation described above. This is used to stave off the fall in profit margin through value created by the circulation of money which produces money and/or by selling debt against debt through very high-risk leverage.

This is not all, however. Finance is having to come to terms with new technologies that were not foreseen 100 years ago. Schumpeter used the term "creative destruction".

New technologies and businesses saw off any technologies and businesses unable to adapt to change, and new surplus value generated by expropriation of surplus labour was created through extended reproduction of the capitalist mechanism—destruction and creation at the same time. This was done not merely by changing the interest rates, as suggested by Keynes, but circulating commodities against commodities as Piero Sraffa envisaged in his *Production of Commodities by means of Commodities*,[7] which is still the best book on economics written in the twentieth century. Now things seem to be changing.

A New Kondratieff Cycle

This has come about because the next approaching Kondratieff cycle has some yet unknown characteristics.

It involves the widespread creation of naturally complex and stratified systems as well as artificial intelligence technologies that engender other intelligences. It is like raising ICT to the nth power. Three-dimensional printers with addition and extrusion mechanisms based on laser technology are just the beginning. The next step will be isomorphic robots existing in a steady state with the human body and with changes in surrounding machinery and the environment.

The outcome is something extraordinarily new, a generalised (not specific, as at one time) fall not merely in highly qualified workers but also in white-collar workers: engineers, physicians and mathematicians. In the past, scanners replaced typesetters and computers replaced typists, secretaries, draughtsmen and designers but this was always specific. Now things will be done on a large scale and will make a clean sweep of millions and millions of graduates and brilliant PhD graduates.

If we then think that the next, great imminent Kondratieff cycle concerns plasma and DNA manipulation, we can be sure that the mutation will be extraordinary. This is much more than an ethical fall from grace, with rampant neopaganism replacing God in creation and love between the sexes in the act of procreation.

Something else is at play. This was apparent to the UK's former Tory Prime Minister David Cameron, when he prevented Pfizer's takeover of AstraZeneca for reasons that were amazing for the tide of ordoliberalism and catastrophic for shareholder value.

Cameron clearly stated that the US Company Pfizer, which produces drugs with no ability to combat new diseases caused by invasive bacteria, would never be allowed to take over AstraZeneca, which fights these invasive diseases through scientific research. In other words, AstraZeneca belonged not only to its shareholders but also to all British universities conducting research against the threat of bacteria.

This threat becomes a reality with growing numbers of migrants harbouring bacteria from all over the world, affecting populations with a very low level of immunity to these foreign threats. I am allowed to say this because I am not standing for election and am certainly immune from racist sympathies of any kind.

But I digress, in this case too, hundreds of thousands of doctors will have to be sent home or on gardening leave as they are replaced by robots and the like: this kind of thing is already happening with remote medicine.

Qualified work is destined to dwindle on a grand scale, opening up a new historical direction.

Other processes are at play. The first is demographic, determined by a global increase in life expectancies and therefore a need for professions to fill the growing need for staff.

As carers are only too well aware, no robots can wash the intimate parts of old people or wipe the drool from Alzheimer's patients with compassion: their mechanical coldness would make death an even sadder affair.

This means that the caring professions, in the widest sense of the word, will grow to cater to the needs of the new centenarians. Nurses will not be enough. We will also have to train readers, jugglers, psychologists and psychiatrists, architects and disseminators of cooperative values to persuade people not to die alone in a spirit of bourgeois individualism but to do it tenderly, taking longer, sharing friendship and love as well as pain, as illustrated by the lovely film by Dustin Hoffmann, *The Quartet*, which everyone should see.

What about finance? Finance can play a very important role because all these activities generate low surpluses and therefore take a very long time to generate profit while requiring immediate investments. Finance can be hugely valuable in such circumstances provided it undergoes a radical change.

Instead of the turbocharged finance of managers with stock options, who are engaged in building hospitals and nursing homes to squeeze more profit out of sickness and death, good finance can play a highly beneficial role, provided the leopard is prepared to change its spots.

The extraordinary Encyclical of Benedict 16th *Caritas in Veritate* on good finance gives us the gist.

All we need to do is take our lead from Jewish philanthropy: the overwhelming majority of Jewish hospitals in the world have already discovered this great truth, just as the cooperative banks have given us a great lesson of hope in the midst of the devastating and disastrous crisis generated by managers with stock options and ordoliberals.

What of the future of work?

Everything we have discussed to this point suggests that financialisation of the capitalist cycle is very likely to produce a counterintuitive effect.

While short-termism and anxiety about dividends cause investments to fall and thus encourage unemployment, three other labour-related spheres herald deep-rooted opposition between social relations of production and productive forces.

The first sphere is that the commodity cycle will always play an irreplaceable role for manual and non-manual, qualified and specialist factory professionals, not merely for managers.

Throughout the world, from Germany to China, there is a shortage of millers, welders, maintenance technicians, chemical engineers and IT engineers. This lack of workers suggests that it will be increasingly difficult to reduce labour to a commodity because workers are bound to become more aware of the value of their efforts.

Another aspect makes the commodification of labour very problematical. Those who remain to carry the torch of science and technology in enterprises and institutions where the processes in question (intelligence and life sciences) will spread will hardly be able to accept salaried employment pure and simple when the jobs they are commanded to perform aim only to squeeze more surplus value.

This phenomenon is already common in high-tech companies, with horizontal organisations, teams and so on. Even if leaders of the cooperative world do not realise it, cutting-edge capitalism ultimately lays claim to principles that are often forgotten.

And what of the huge mass of skilled, qualified workers who will have to look after people and care for them? Can such work be done without compassion, an intimate understanding of pain and of the struggle to overcome it?

All this can only lay the basis for transcending full-on capitalist management to allow the survival of human beings: the wounded, fragile, hurting people who are about to shuffle off this mortal coil.

Does this financial or non-financial future therefore lay the basis for transcending the idea of labour as commodity?

The sentry is waiting in the night. The call will come.

A Technology for Long-term Stagnation?

Expectations are ruled by growing fantasies about the new technological and digital age.

There is a lot of talk about digital revolution.

Enzo Rullani[8] envisages a combined cognitive and transformative model, a kind of global fourth industrial revolution.

Digital platforms and supply chains mean the future has already arrived. Transaction costs have also been lowered in time and space by the use of machinery that works by additive manufacturing instead of by ablation and extrusion. For approximately 20 years, the new manufacturing production supply chain has been employing a growing group of operators in technology clusters to reduce industrial costs and extend working practices determined by changes affecting various technological and productive supply chains: a new technology has arrived for a new type of capitalism.

This new Kondatrieff wave is the driving force behind the contemporary world, not finance. It takes place through a dual process: disseminating production sites and immeasurably expanding the reliability and quality of products and processes.

The latter process is the outcome of 20 years of work conducted by various technological research centres on materials. The latest discovery has revealed rare earths to be revolutionary materials based on initial findings in the field of nanotechnology.

These results, combined with research on magnetic fields, lasers and non-ethylene chemistry, have led to manufacturing techniques that work through addition and not ablation or extrusion, with surprising results on technology and quality control.

Great changes have also come about through high-level research into mechatronics, and an entire universe of machinery has been created to produce machines, products and prototypes with multiple versatile qualities that are known as 3-D printers.

These have allowed decentralisation of production, prototyping and reproduction to order and on a very large scale, with a consequent reduction in material constraints affecting transaction costs in time and space.

The consequences for the future of human labour and for permanent and temporary human settlements will be enormous.

The innovations allow new potential for a return to production in urban areas, for example, as a consequence of lower environmental impact and reduced layout requirements.

An incredible level of production and distribution decentralisation is possible on a global scale, and new geopolitical scenarios will arise due to relocating innovative manufacturing and the control of new materials, alloys, composite and powder metallurgy.

The convergence of these incremental discoveries, which have gone hand in hand with the development of machinery for the production of ever more intelligent machines, can bring about a revolution in the quality of work ordered and the type of fixed and variable capital that will be required to make the change irreversible.

A new civilisation based on new machinery seems to be just over the horizon.

This requires a new metaphysical training and strategic approach that addresses the spirit of the times.

Instead, everything is aimed at grasping the reductionist economic aspects of the current process.

In aerospace manufacturing—another sector affected—progress is already a reality and the consequences are evident in terms of product development, work distribution, qualifications and skills mix, reliability and timing made possible by the technological potential of "AM" (Additive Manufacturing).

We need to take a step back to really understand what is happening.

In 1984, the people at Verlag Bech in Munich published a text that for a long time represented a single point of reference for the very few who wished to understand the link between work and technological development based on manufacture: *Das Ende der Arbeiststeilung? Rationalisierung in der industriellen Produktion.*[9]

The authors were two great sociologists working at the University of Gottingen Soziologisches Forschunginstitut: Horst Kern and Michael Schuman.

The aim of their study was to see whether they could come up with a way of forecasting the future of work delivered as part of a capitalist added-value relationship. The research project was based on the conviction that ex-post reasoning is not enough to implement the best transformations achieved during the course of living work—workers and technicians in their professional and psychological training, and dead work—technologies put into practice in working establishments.

Their ambitions were very similar to those guiding Taylor's pioneering studies at the dawn of the "scientific organisation of labour",[10] in other words to combine high productivity of work with the best ergonomic conditions for workers' lives at the human-machinery interface.

It is interesting to find that problems typical of the early 1980s, which preceded the big spurt during the "new economy" years when there were no cyclic recessions in the US economy for approximately a decade that surrounded the start of a major new Kondatrieff[11] cycle, were the same as today. Now another such cycle is unfolding in all its breadth, beginning with technological innovation lowering transaction costs relating to time and space factors (the Schumpeterian emergence of ICT in the capitalist cycle).

This book seeks to explain the similarities and differences between these two technological waves (the term "revolution"[12] is too problematic and imprecise).

The central idea of the essay by Horst and Schuman is that the technological process completely lost its innocence (during those years), and events did not amount to deindustrialisation, as many pseudo-academics from around the world argued with great fanfare, but rather a colossal process of neo-industrialisation.

This reflection is centred on the assumption that the Taylorist practice of mass production was beginning to crumble. It was replaced by another type of high-volume production made possible by a rationalisation that increased labour automation and robotisation, transforming the role of mechanical and electronic supply chains.

The importance of this phenomenon was apparent, but it was impossible to fully grasp the dynamics of change. The cause of this lay in the assumption central to that seminal analysis.

This assumption was as follows: the changes were being brought about by the transformation of labour and not the transformation of machinery. Labour was contracting yet becoming more professional. In other words, blue-collar workers tended to disappear and be replaced by technical operators working on increasingly complex machinery that they regulated rather than operated.

Specialist workers (the analytical link chosen by the authors) were studied to establish whether they felt defensive about processes that they did not control but undoubtedly interpreted and went along with.

The basic idea was far ahead of its time.

Horst and Schuman discussed a form of production rationalisation that advanced through successive, increasingly intense waves that took away work while increasing its complexity.

As today, change centred on transformations of and within machine tools that remain the framework of transformation in every sense: within labour and dead capital, that is machinery and plant.

Mechanical engineering was naturally the slowest part of this process of automation. The process was streets ahead in the chemical industry where automation was part and parcel of the manufacturing process and organisation was incorporated in technology with much higher rates of determinism than those present in mechanical engineering.

The change was becoming increasingly significant, with the use of built-in automation equipment and growing differentiation of performance required of workers-operators. A system of mechanical maintenance poised between stasis, and movement completely changed the relationship between maintenance staff and direct production staff, leading to a blurring of professional tasks and profiles.

The two academics observed that partial automation was proceeding by leaps and bounds in all industries, starting from manufacturing and relatively independent of the corporate dimension.

As part of this process, they saw the colossal change due to take place in the ICT age would definitively release an entire series of production services and some stages of production from the corporate dimension in the strict sense.

Polarisation between skilled workers and labourers was being replaced by a new world of classifications and qualifications. This was ruled by ad hoc segmentation defined on the basis of the interaction between professional training and breadth of machine production, in other words the intersection of various production supply chains (the breadth) in the dynamics of manufacture, beginning with machines working in the plants.

This paved the way for further investigations: focusing on changes in machinery in order to understand labour, as we try to do today and as I will attempt to do in this book.

The stage that is opening up over the last two or three years is continuous with the processes I have discussed briefly yet marks a radical break with the past.

In attempting to outline these processes, we can draw on two works that I advise reading together even though they are apparently unrelated.[13]

The most relevant question concerns the spread of technology. We are not interested merely in the spread within and between manufacturing machinery supply chains. The thing at stake is the spread of machines throughout all our everyday lives.

Although this notion appears extemporaneous, I believe it will take on an essential significance. This spread is based on the principle of Moore's Law: in 1965, Gordon Moore (an IT specialist who was very influential at the time) came up with his law when he noticed that the number of transistors on a chip doubled every year while the costs were halved. This meant that processors would soon be 500 times more powerful without costing any more.[14] This implied that integrated circuits would allow home computers, as they were called in those days, to automatically control cars and portable communication tools if they were connected to central computers.

Moore's principle establishes that the power of processors doubles every 18 months while their prices are halved.

No invention or innovation has ever increased its power at such a rapid rate in the history of humanity: the computer's power increases exponentially while the computer itself becomes increasingly cheap and potentially more accessible.

The Watson supercomputer made by IBM in 2011 is clear proof. It was built to understand language well and was therefore able to identify correspondences and use increasingly complex communication skills. It was intended to improve on the Deep Blue model that managed to beat the world chess champion Garry Kasparov in 1997 in their second game. Nowadays a fairly commonly available smart phone can be loaded with an app able to replicate that victory, proving the truth of Moore's law.

Automatic learning has brought some impressive successes. This is because a computer's algorithms allow it to improve on its own ability to forecast and analyse. It is an impressive use of statistics: the computer learns the probable answer by trial and error, and this process is becoming increasingly rapid and surprising as a result of Moore's law. It is no longer a question of putting hundreds of decryption experts to work (as was done up to 20 or so years ago) and getting them to copy word lists and then search for significant matches in translation. Nowadays an automatic programme can quickly and systematically compare texts in various languages to find the most likely matches with another language and thus come up with a huge and ever-expanding database of corresponding texts.

This explains why Brynjolfsson and McAfee claim that we are faced with a game-changing technological innovation that, as I said, can trigger a gigantic new Kondratieff-style innovation cycle.

The power and versatility of computers can now change entire significant segments of human activity within and without manufacturing.

This has been a fairly recent change and their use in robotics is a striking example of this. We are all aware of the paradigm of robots being controlled by computer programming: they can do things that are difficult for humans to do very well but are unable to do things that are easy for humans.

Is this still true? We know that computers find it difficult if not impossible to implement SLAM. SLAM stands for "simultaneous localisation and mapping". This means being able to see a space, learn to live inside it, memorise this capacity and replicate it. This type of activity is crucial to robotics, but for years, computers have been unable to learn how to be good at SLAM. Films show the most sophisticated robots stumbling when they attempt to take two steps. However, Moore's law has come up trumps again in this field, so crucial for the transformation of machines. A visit to any sophisticated industrial warehouse says it all. Kiva robots trundle around warehouses, lifting packs and objects weighing dozens of kilograms. They are remotely controlled along pre-established paths that they gradually learn so well that they are able to change course if they encounter process changes, then resume their learned route once the disruption has been removed, gradually improving their knowledge.

Much of e-commerce could not exist without this improved processor capacity.

Localisation is still a practical problem We can automate entire product chains, filling the most sophisticated jars and vials with the most varied selection of liquids and foods, but if the vials or jars wobble, computers and robots go into meltdown because they cannot reformulate the localisation in real time, however millions of algorithms they automatically crunch.

I am convinced that Moore's law will be borne out in this field too: it is merely a question of time.

Horst and Schuman's predictive paradigm suggests that labour will be replaced by automated machines, and skilled workers will have to become sophisticated operators who would be classified using as yet un-formulated protocols.

A world involving the self-production of increasingly sophisticated algorithms poses the problem of eliminating human labour from manufacturing, not merely transforming it.

Moore's law means we are now no longer faced with the problem of automating, privatising and doing away with low-skilled workers.

New smart machines and manufacturing models able to overcome SLAM-related risks mean that the ongoing requirement for very highly skilled workers is also being called into question.

This was demonstrated by Brynjolfsson and McAfee. The book by these two authors was as much of a scientific milestone as the work by the two German academics in the 1980s and 1990s. Its premise is that we must begin to conceive of a future where smart machines replace not only workers performing repetitive tasks on a large industrial scale but also the clerks and technicians working within the industries as well as the services and processes contributing non-repetitive, creative and non-creative components to the resulting working time.

Tyler Coven[15] has explained how this process will have important consequences on income distribution. Those able to interact with the new smart machines will receive the lion's share of the income.

A new age of capitalist development will open up before our eyes, but we might not be aware of it.

The crux of the matter is that if we assume this process to be the new all-round paradigm and it incorporates what is commonly meant when we refer to income and wages or salary distribution in Ricardian terms, we have not touched on the topic of labour productivity, which is increasingly assumed as a transparent paradigm of distribution and wages when formulating a Ricardian added-value process.

In the neoclassical model of exogenous growth by Solow,[16] he assumed that the triggering factor was always the technological process, which overdetermines shares of labour and capital input ("Solow's residue"). However, he stated that new innovations generated by microprocessors and therefore by the processes referred to above have little relevance in raising productivity.

Solow stated that the new innovation model did not fit his model. Tellingly, his model is unable to explain the level of growth in output, that is productivity, while maintaining labour and capital constant.

Robert Gordon[17] went one step further in a recent fascinating and in some respects terrifying work comparing productivity growth rates resulting from the second industrial revolution (1870–1900), which was triggered by the invention of the internal combustion engine, the dynamo, the telephone and so on.

These innovations radically transformed the lives of tens of millions of people and still underpin the organisation of production as well as the reproduction of society. The same thing happened at the beginning of the computer and electronic age, which many of us alive today experienced.

The succession of change processes induced by exponential application of the discoveries made during that initial age did not have significant consequences for productivity, according to Gordon, but did influence the level of consumption and its differentiation.

Firstly, they had an impact on leisure that is entertainment and our use of time not to work but to amuse ourselves or, worse still, to distract our attention and destroy our ability to concentrate.

According to Gordon, Moore's law gave rise to an explosion of mostly useless innovations that have destroyed labour faster than it can be created in new and different sectors, as has always been the case throughout all technological ages and changes to the economic structure of society.[18]

Would we be able to cope with the kind of social transformations induced by the gigantic process of replacing agricultural work by the industrial and services sectors, which began at the beginning of the twentieth century at an unequal rate all over the world? Gordon's question is frightening.

Although he believes that the technological revolution brought about by smart machines has already happened, the authors Brynjolfsson and McAfee think very differently. They believe that the revolution has yet to take place or rather has only just begun. They equate it to events during the first Industrial Revolution, when inventions were followed by a long period of waiting. In other words, the changes could not be applied until certain requirements that were more socioeconomic than technological had been fulfilled. This is clear to anyone who goes back to the rudiments, which are not statistical (unfortunately everything seems to be about statistics these days) but social and anthropological observations drawn from economic history.

If this is true, as I believe, that the smart machine revolution is just beginning, the first results suggest that the future of work will not be unlike that suggested by Horst and Schuman.

Firstly, with regard to the effects on employment, we need to reflect on statements made by Frey and Osborne in a paper published in Oxford, which I believe to be a seminal work. This is explicitly entitled[19]: *The future of employment: How susceptible are jobs to computerisation?*

Briefly describing 722 present-day forms of employment, the authors give us a vision of the future based on their predictions of the jobs that will be the most important. In crude terms, they tell us which jobs will exist in the future, while all others are destined to disappear.

The first five jobs that the authors believe will take precedence over all others are: recreational therapists, mechanical supervisors, installers and repairers, emergency activity managers, social operators in the field of mental health and audiologists.

In the detailed classification, we can read with a certain amount of apprehension which jobs the authors believe will be the rarest: insurers, mathematical technicians, tailors, notaries and accountants, call centre operators.

The message we can take from this study is that all jobs based on interpersonal and emotional relationships and on capabilities and technologies for maintaining complex artificial and intelligent systems will remain and even increase until they take over. All occupations with a strong impersonal mechanical component, whatever the technological complexity (even surgeons, e.g., will be lower in number than choreographers), will dwindle until they disappear.

Financial services, business services, routine legal professions as well as operators running machine tools at all levels will gradually be eliminated without mercy.

The prevailing current myth that the most important thing required to keep or find a job is a good level of training attained in an excellent college (for a fat fee) will collapse. Frey and Osborne have a stab at predicting the figures: within 20 years, 47% of jobs will fall into the category of jobs at such a high risk of obsolescence that they risk disappearing. In recent decades, jobs requiring mid-level qualifications have declined while those with very low levels of qualification and ultra-high levels of complexity have increased. In the future, smart machines will determine the end of less specialised, no-waged jobs.

The future will be made up of wealthy people who have no problems, middle classes who can get by and poor people for whom there is no hope.

This trend can be confirmed by observing events in the North American world of work. Unlike those who do not believe that the advent of new machines will increase productivity, Frey and Osborne believe the opposite and that this growth in productivity will always exceed mid-level wages and increase wealth for upper social classes.

Even though the quantity of living work is reduced, this should bring about an exponential growth in surplus value and therefore a dizzying increase in social differentiation, as is already evident today when we observe life scrolling before our eyes.

Machines will be owned by 0.1% of the population, 0.9% will manage them and 99% will be employed in the small amount of non-automated work available or will languish in the pits of unemployment.

We are also witnessing a radical transformation in the mechanism of accumulation. Capital is no longer accumulated by companies such as General Electric or by General Motors but instead by companies like Apple and the like.

The real difference lies in the fact that the first two companies mentioned above have provided jobs for hundreds of thousands of workers all over the world, while companies such as Apple and Google employ a few tens of thousands and are slashing their staff numbers.

The increase in productivity allowed by machines greatly increases the massive surplus value with an incredible increase in differentiation and increasingly disturbing social polarisation.

When we consider that discoveries, currently the prerogative of companies such as Google or Apple, are beginning to take root in traditional companies such as General Electric or General Motors, the consequences appeared to be exactly those predicted by Frey and Osborne: Google is working to build a driverless car and this technology is already a reality in many metros operating throughout the world.

Technological and social trends can only reinforce theories of long-term stagnation induced by growing deflation. Such theories are now essential for understanding the world economy and stem from the scientific work of the great Alvin Hansen[20]: a powerful Keynesian economist before the term was even invented, who wrote his works—which were similar to those of his illustrious colleague—at the same time but never rose to the same heights of fame.

Deflation caused by a collapse in the price of raw materials due to the apparently prevailing productive overcapacity in BRICS will be joined by deflation caused by the collapse of the wage bill and hence of domestic demand, according to the forecasts of Frey and Osborne.

The consequences could be devastating, and we could have a long and lonely wait for the smart machine revolution to replace the effective demand for income from work using resources other than financial resources, whose therapeutic qualities are now in any case questioned by all prevailing theories.

The falling prices of goods produced using the technical innovations discussed here would not, in my opinion, halt long-term stagnation and would thwart the potential wealth of opportunities that smart machines offer on the social front, almost as though they were a two-faced Janus looking to the future and to the past.

The capitalist mechanisms would clash with production relationships if it failed—as some hope—to overcome the bottleneck of social polarisation.

If this bottleneck is not removed, it is unclear who will buy the immense quantity of goods produced using the anticipated innovations.

The longer-term, broader implications of the advent of new machines concern the intimate structure of social relations that we all too often avoid addressing.

We are faced with what John Lanchester[21] termed a "hyper-capitalist dystopia", encapsulating an inescapable internal contradiction if current property rights allocation models remain as they are.

Mechanics, Commodities, Labour

Moving from a general overview to a more detailed and specific examination of the technological changes in progress, we inevitably come face to face with the heart of the change, which is enclosed in the iron cage of mechanical manufacturing.

Some academics have approached the matter in highly original ways but travelled the same pathway as Horst and Schuman by making any consequences that the change has already had and changes it will have in the future on human work and its characteristics central to their analysis.

Martin Ford made the most fascinating contribution to the debate.[22] He embraces the matter of the relationship between education and work and busts the widespread myth among the middle classes that a good education will smooth your path to a good job: does attending a good college still guarantee you a good job?

Everything hinges on the concept of nuances. Can we really be sure that only the human brain is capable of dealing with interactive and sophisticated work operations that require continuous adaptability to the outside world, whether technical or human? Ford believes that this ability is increasingly expressible as an algorithm, in other words a capacity that we once believed could be achieved only through increasingly sophisticated academic hurdles that the human mind has had to face by passing tougher and tougher exams at a top university. However, computers are increasingly solving problems of this type with impressive speed and capacity for change.

It has been predicted that even writing based on ideation can be carried out by well-trained machines that think as well as write.... Book reviews, for example, can be written by automatic procedures that gradually improve with practice. Text scanning leads to algorithmic processing that precedes the ability to map, read and even interpret increasingly broad series of publishing products that until now were produced by a sophisticated human mind previously thought to be irreproducible except through an education based on a classic humanist philosophy.

According to this approach, mass non-employment or semi-employment becomes a not-too-distant prospect and not only for specific segments or specific working supply chains with a high cognitive content. If we believe this, we must believe what we discussed earlier in the first part of the essay, namely that not producing living labour becomes a corporate strategy implicit in the adoption of new technologies from the start of the product life-cycle. Schumpeter's business cycles[23] become an alarming set of phenomena that are increasingly devoid of human labour despite their innovative aspects.

We have never given this aspect due consideration.

When Ford wished to describe the change brought about by machines, he could not avoid referring to changes in manufacturing: "New industries will rarely, if ever, be highly labour-intensive, pointing to companies like You Tube and Instagram, which are characterised by tiny work-forces and huge valuation and revenues. On another front 3D printing is poised to make a mockery of manufacturing as we knew it. Truck driving may survive for a while—at least until self-driving vehicles start rolling out of Detroit or, perhaps, San Jose".[24]

What escapes authors like Ford and too many others to mention here is that the process of deconstructing labour evident at the surface of the new industrial society is based on a process that is quite the opposite of deconstruction. Instead, it is a process of constructing and reconstructing a series of machines that are the creative and non-algorithmic consequence of intersections between complex technological (and therefore cognitive, human) supply chains.

New manufacturing unearths a deep-rooted process that I attempted to describe years ago during my 20-year-long study of technological transformations in Italian industry,[25] which has now been enormously enhanced on a global scale through the changes described previously.

These changes affect the socioeconomic system and not merely the industrial and scientific system.

Mechatronics lies at the root of everything. This is the intertwining of three great technological strands: mechanics, electronics and information technologies.

It has many areas of application and in a certain sense it is as infinite as the number of human needs and the technological and scientific resources we can call on today to meet these needs and new inventions springing from human creativity.

The enormous algorithmic capacity actually helps rather than hinders.

It acts as an enormous lever for extending such cognitive applications indefinitely.

They include automotive, avionics and aeronautics, transport, biomedicine, energy and all forms of industrial machinery, particularly robots, agricultural and food technology, from the most complex domotics to buildings of all shapes and complexities.

Decentralisation, virtualisation, modularity and interoperability as well as the crucial function of prototyping are simply a combination of tools and applications that increasingly transform the technical, socioeconomic and human environment in which they are embedded.[26]

In other words, they are the outcome and causes of the shape civil society is gradually assuming: technological and any other form of innovation could not exist without such causes. Grannovetter and Magatti have written fine, enlightening works on this embedding and immersion that we should always keep in mind, particularly when talking about machines—smart and otherwise, but particularly if they are smart…

If we bear in mind what has been stated so far in this section, perhaps the future of work might not be quite so tragic.

Moving on, there is now a general multidisciplinary, analytical consensus that the connection point of all these supply chains and technological and social applications is additive manufacturing, normally referred to as 3-D printing.

The most enlightening work in this field was written by Pasquale Alferj and Alessandra Favazzo[27] and I wholeheartedly recommend readers to refer to it and reflect on the most significant points.

The fact that this article describes the activities of a company that has used smart machines as a business idea only makes this contribution more interesting.

This idea is the quintessential core of additive manufacturing, promoting its application and then allowing this innovation to become the driving force behind a Schumpeter-style business cycle as discussed previously.

The key issue is once again the lowering of transaction costs.

Using additive manufacturing makes it possible to speed up production and sales by reaching out directly to end customers, overcoming multiple forms of commercial intermediation and blurring the divisions between design and production until they disappear, and design, prototyping and production become one. The structure of the commodity is already entirely defined in three-dimensional mathematical models contained in computers allowing goods to be manufactured by printing them at a site that is often close to the user. Modelling lies at the centre of design and manufacture, through the use of digital technologies and alphanumerical control of machines of varying complexity controlled by operators who may employ different styles to deliver their work but are nevertheless an integral part of the control activity.

Nowadays, a central role is played by additive technologies that give a profound sense of the manufacturing transformation introduced by machines that work not by ablation or extrusion but by addition: an additive mechanical process that is built up layer by layer based on a computer-aided design shaped by a three-dimensional mathematical process.

A crucial role is played by research into materials that can be used for additive technologies, including fused ABS plastic, liquid resins, titanium, aluminium, alloys, ceramics and glass. I will return to this topic later.

None of this would be possible without fused deposition models and selective laser technologies. Rapid printing and prototyping techniques have played an impressively important and vigorous role, ensuring high-quality sintered materials and fast manufacturing. This allows the option of limited series that can be continued for mass production. The ensuing previously unthinkable industrial cycles can be used to make sturdy yet light components that could be part of practically unlimited series offering exceptional yields considering the temperatures and stresses induced by weight and friction.

Many multinationals now have impressive systems to apply additive manufacturing models in contexts where performances must be precise and the system, production and delivery timing must be absolutely foolproof. The workforce must be superlatively well-trained to ensure its quality and capacity for adaptation and continuous improvement.

This is what we should be emphasising, instead of complaining there is not enough work.

As yet, there are no empirical studies in this field. These would be very interesting and effective in giving us a realistic and non-apocalyptic view of the new industrial society being opened up by additive manufacturing.

The Californian Makers movement that has been so successful, particularly in Italy and Germany, borne on a wave of neo-Luddite and superstitious ecological ideologies, is greatly distorting the direction of change and its enormously complex and generally positive implications.

This prevalently gloomy ecological and pseudo craft-centred view conceals the true significance of the current Kondratieff cycle: a new form of mass production and a new great industry that greatly enhances the technological and scientific achievements available today, whatever their social production relationships.

This is not at all at odds with a revival of Renaissance craftsmanship[28]: additive manufacturing now extends to small and micro-enterprises with extremely positive consequences. The same thing applies to industrial neo-urbanisation processes that can generate employment and redesign opportunities in an intertwining of art and industry that we believed was a thing of the past.

Nowadays it can be resurrected with wonderful consequences and implications for a return to a humanist vision of industry irrespective of ownership or size.

Customisation of production goes hand in hand with the impact on inventories, delivery times and so on, beginning with the Internet of things, which involves designing goods and commodities that can be interconnected at all stages of design and production via the Internet in real time.

Digital planning does not detract from manual skills but enhances them.

I used the term "embedded technology" in a cognitive and emotional sense typical of the origins of every mechanical and digital form of processing, which I personally experienced when young and that has now forcefully come full cycle … humanising the algorithm.

It was a real struggle in the beginning. Anyone who talks to the pioneers of these iconic innovations understands how difficult it has been to interface technologies and materials as diverse as optics, electronics, materials chemistry, electrosynthesis and powdered materials with ultra-high-temperature laser technologies, with software models and … mechanics: dear old mechanics rising from its ashes after all this time.

All this has been happening under difficult conditions in a market—or rather several markets—that have developed during these years of recession in fractal-like form, in other words perennially variable and unstable.

Entrepreneurial ingenuity is all the more essential with 3-D printers and technologies.

They have a secret soul and we all need to get to know it better.

Soul of the Capitalist Machinery

The hidden heart of technological growth is still the most mysterious aspect of the current hi-tech revolution: something that the great master Nathan Rosenberg referred to as the black box of the company and civil society, responsible for the embeddedness of technological development.[29]

Additive manufacturing has its own black box and we need to begin to shed light on it from within.

We have already said that the cornerstone of this technology is the speed and accuracy of prototyping processes.

It has been a long struggle, an ongoing accumulation: I feel these are incremental innovations of the type described by Marshall[30] rather than paradigm-shifting technological and scientific revolutions of the type described by Khun.[31]

Rapid prototyping lies at the heart of innovation due to additive mechanics.

A very important work by Kruth, Leu and Nakagawa tackles this matter from a broad range of perspectives that is decisive for understanding the foundations of my incrementalist theory.[32]

According to the authors, who revealed the international nature of the research when they opened up their work for scrutiny by the scientific community (they were based at the universities of Leuven, New Jersey and Tokyo, respectively), it took approximately a decade of work from the end of the 1980s to the end of the 1990s to achieve good-enough results to establish rapid prototyping processes through a series of continuous increments in executive speed.

The authors posed themselves the problem of achieving an operational interface between electrophysical and chemical processes aimed at allowing the addition of alternative materials selected for manufacture based on specific productive needs. From chemical to thermophysical processes, from liquid injection to solid addition, culminating in the use of ultrasonic instruments: their aim was to create additive processes through stereolithography and thermal induction using lasers that synthesise and process plasma. They reproduced synthetic electrolytic processes to meet requirements and ultimately initiated 3-D printing procedures.

Polymers, non-ferrous materials, rare earth and ceramics were used alternately in the prototyping procedure. Everything was achieved through the use of a number of complex mechatronic systems that were painstakingly classified.

Laser modelling immediately assumed immense importance together with the support software, software concepts and learning processes that had to be poured into processes and systems as and when required.

The technical materials submitted reflect incessant work on individual production and design stages that this study (together with other significant works) documents with a scrupulousness that we cannot go into here.

Many metallurgy and materials engineering laboratories have been working for decades on the manufacture of new metal alloys and the design of new techniques for using lasers, up to the formidable progress achieved in electron beam melting (EBM) technologies that create an energy source in the form of a concentrated and accelerated beam of electrons that strikes a material in microgranulometric manner, causing its complete fusion. From pure metal to the powdered state, full finished parts are produced by positioning powdered layers of the material to be fused under a vacuum, which can mean working on materials that immediately react with oxygen.

Everything takes place between 700 and 1000 °C, to obtain parts that essentially lack residual stress, thus avoiding the need for heat treatment after the production process.[33]

Control of metal deposition processes through analysis of their microstructures and the mechanical properties has played a decisive role that must never be underestimated: it opens a scientific and technological chain starting from geological research and culminating in the most sophisticated design and engineering and mechanical-chemical production techniques.[34]

All this increases the knowledge of three-dimensional implementation processes, in all their physical and mechanical variants.[35] Three-dimensionality and mapping, together with gradual progress in laser equipment design, have been decisive technological achievements, stretching from the 1970s in a never-ending process of improvement that is still ongoing.[36]

The essential secret of every technological, organisational or cognitive process lies in its execution or implementation.

Valuable contributions have been made in this field. Perhaps, the most interesting is one made by the University of Exeter, where a group of academics has been working on the matters that interest us for years.[37]

> With over 20 years of history, in its early years AM was mostly applied for the fabrication of conceptual and functional prototypes, also known as Rapid Prototyping(RP) These prototypes used as communication and inspection tools, producing several physicals models in short time directly from computer solid models help to shorten the production development steps. RP remains the dominant application of polymer AM process and is well established in the market. More of aforementioned technologies are limited to Rapid Prototyping as they do not allow common engineering materials to be processed with sufficient mechanical properties (polymers, metals, ceramics and composite thereof) The concept of Rapid Manufacturing (RM)-the production of end use parts from AD systems remain modest. There are few large scale applications of RM, many of which are for producing personalised products in the medical field.... The aerospace sector has also found a number of applications, often driven by the possibility of improving buy to fly ratios ... and reducing the weight of components through design optimisation. Other areas include automotive, jewellery, architecture and defence applications.[38]

According to the authors (two of whom were writing in 2014), the main obstacle to the wider circulation of AM, apart from market conditions, is a lack of sufficient: "technical standards ... a major barrier to adoption. Some of these characteristics of AM are likely due to their relative immaturity and managers should be aware of this when deciding whether to adopt."[39]

The conclusions to the research conducted by the Exeter academics therefore aim at implementing a change—which they are unable to perceive but are aware is important—in organisational concepts governing the implementation of processes supplied in and by AM. These do not yet actually exist. They are feeling their way in the dark.

This challenge is opening up before us and now is the time for the major enterprises that will adopt the techniques and technologies described here to start their research.

From human beings who invent we are therefore going back to being human beings who decide what machines do and ultimately what part human beings play in the world.

Every day.

This is why we must go back to studying workers and employees.

Why Should We Research Workers and Employees Today?

Because labour and technology grow and feed through cross-contamination. The role of mass workers disappeared with the passing of the Taylor and Ford model. This also marked the passing of types of industrial conflict inherent in mass production as it emerged from the changes that began at the turn of the twentieth century and continued throughout the century in countries that adopted this approach to manufacturing. This change also obliterated all left-wing class struggle stereotypes.

These days, knowledge workers are not solely white-collar workers (or a proportion of these) but often (and possibly more entitled to this definition) blue-collar workers; this insight should lead us to review the entire category of knowledge workers.

Because the values, stimuli, motivations and behaviour of the new working class (manufacturing workers) are quite different in new generations (the Y generation) compared to previous generations, just as symbolic models, best practices, work ethics and forms of identification with the company are also different. This also applies to the impact of the change on the professional, personal and social sphere.

Any survey into contemporary employees with the aim of coming up with a well-founded, sound knowledge of what distinguishes the behavioural and value models of new generations of dependent workers (unevenly and randomly distributed between life time and temporary workers) must therefore prioritise the choice of research method.

In other words, if the choice of method always depends on what one is attempting to discover, a qualitative analysis is the most appropriate way of exploring the practices of people at work, whatever form this relationship between people and work may take.

Action guidelines are based on an immense and very uneven universe of desires and values, beliefs and information.

The real strength of a qualitative analysis is that it uses spontaneous data (e.g. by connecting life stories and unstructured interviews) to reconstruct sequences that build up a meaningful picture of the stakeholders.

The ethnographic and storytelling side of the research reflects a theoretical interest in finding out how people learn to know, do and decide: it acknowledges that nowadays "common sense" is often much more complex and sophisticated than simple trial and error; it also acknowledges that "practice" (much more than "perception") is the true home of common sense and the research is therefore much more attentive to what people *do* than what they think.

Given the current instability, corporate systems are increasingly culture-dependent. Acknowledging a need for change does not always mean that those who plan changes prioritise the deciphering of corporate cultures that influence the change and by which they in turn are influenced.

Culture (or rather the mix of different cultures that always coexist in a business, particularly a large one) is often the crucial factor: many breakthrough projects fail even if they are perfectly designed from a financial, technological and strategic viewpoint, because they fail to take account of people (and their implicit and explicit assumptions, mental maps, prescriptive requirements and behavioural modulations). The reasons for failure can easily be attributed to hard factors, but the reasons for success invariably have a major and powerful catalyst (even though it is not always evident): the qualities of people working in the organisation and their convergence towards shared goals.

The ability to build organisations that constantly respond to change is what matters most today: this means the ability to anticipate the reading of scenarios and the ability to govern unpredictable external stresses acting on the organisation, people, technologies, knowledge and the company culture. The unknown factor is being able to keep up with changes in strategy and structure, people, anthropological and non-manipulative changes in the populations developing the processes used to produce goods and services.

The fundamental role of corporate management nowadays is not so much concerned with competence and control but with facilitating change with the aim of achieving operational excellence: management is really always about change management, and corporate management must be consistently revitalised. A strategy emerges from several items: flexibility (which always involves attention to history and sharing practices) becomes a primary factor, companies must see themselves as complex learning systems.

Change presupposes learning and learning presupposes learning organisation: hence cultural creation (of the values and symbols assumed) and design of learning processes (once the internal and external forces driving change have been understood); structures aiming at personal growth, systemic thinking and tolerance and acceptance of error; the maps required for this purpose must plot the nature of interactions within and between different organisational units, forms of language used and information flow channels, research strategies, spaces for "noise" (different ideas and perspectives)—learning is a self-organisational phenomenon that must be facilitated and regulated.

Management planning has lost the illusion of enlightenment that accompanied it for so long: nowadays we must constantly analyse the strategic issue that has a real-time impact on company management: the systemic metaphor of learning organisation describes the common viewpoint of participants, based on generative conversations and shared actions in a communal, bottom-up process and opens up spaces for learning. It rejects fragmentary thought and embraces common memory, based on an idea of the generative power of language and a refusal to seek absolute truth but rather to rely on consistent interpretations.[40]

This general reflection on organisational culture is remarkable for the long-standing absence of any analysis of the significant universe of working populations who make up the existing manufacturing structure in most major economic nations, who have built up industrial societies over the years and now make up the new working class in the globalised world due to the enormous percentage growth of the new working class in emerging nations.

While workers employed in the industries of emerging countries are an entirely new phenomenon, the reproduction of workers' settlements in traditional manufacturing site settlement areas is a very different matter, due to the overlapping and intermingling of different generations of workers who radically reclassify the mix of cultures passing through the workers' symbolic space.

Having rejected the classicist paradigms of a monolithic work culture, which is the result of political and trade union ideology rather than the lived experience of work and workers, the new working class coexists with previous generations. It is an essential field of analysis for building an understanding that is not merely scientifically neutral but managerially operational within the social and cultural relationships present in modern factories, driven to change under the pressure of increasingly sophisticated factory technologies and management techniques introduced in recent years.

An analysis of working-class cultures is essential because of the operational implications and to provide a means of dealing more effectively with those cultures.

Any cultural analysis of organisations hinges around two main points: a description and an interpretation.

The first point could be a description of the history and current operation of a manufacturing site in a different and more effective form than is commonly used, which is always based on the analytical relevance of workers' behaviours, values and cultures.

It is a shame that the age of blue-collar worker surveys, which made such important contributions in the 1950s and 1960s, has come to an end,[41] because their absence is felt in the radically different current scenario; on the other hand, manufacturing industry is often and somewhat over-hastily said to be spent or expatriated and the "workers" seem to assume it has disappeared altogether. More generally, there are still far too few regular empirical surveys on the way daily practices and social relations have been changed by the radical innovations introduced by what is known as the new economy, at least in Italy.[42] We must reclaim a multi-perspective view of factories. This was the approach taken at one time by many middle managers in industry and some of them still use this strategy, but their voices are not heard and all too often, they are not even prompted or sought. We need to investigate the peripheral rationalism of those who drive the machinery, highlighting the way this is internally organised from the management to the worker base, the local area and the external environment. We also need to explain the rationalism of the centre: in other words, the planning done by managers and those capable of seeing things from the viewpoint of the organisation as a whole.

The second point on which the research hinges is therefore a systemic interpretation of the interaction between the plant and central structures in order to spot virtuous cycles or unexpected and detrimental interruptions. This will enable us to understand how an organisation can respond to change quickly and adequately, essentially because it is capable of generative communication and shared action in relation to shared goals and what stands in the way of these processes.

Rethinking the situation of employed workers nowadays means overcoming the dramatic and solitary fate of workers, who are no longer studied using interactive, dynamic methods that enhance their professional awareness and develop their potential for cognitive competencies and skills and experiential know-how.

Scientific research would be of great importance due to the managerial repercussions I have underlined as well as the intrinsic civil values of such research, which would increase the reputation of the company sponsoring and supporting it with intellectual freedom.

Many preconceptions would certainly be swept away.

One example is the political participation of blue-collar workers and employees. The structural invariance of their social situation in the face of cultural changes affecting this set of social classes is striking.

For example, workers are registered and actively participate in the life of trade unions that are traditionally located in a political subculture different from the one to which the workers refer when they vote in elections.

This phenomenon is as old as the hills. The writings of the few great social scientists who have given it any attention are still extremely apt: some enlightened publisher should republish them. One example is Sombart,[43] who wondered at the beginning of the twentieth century why socialism would never gain a foothold (it never has) in North America.

I also remember the writings of one of the few great masters I admired in my youth, who was mocked by the pundits of '68 in Italy: Theodor

Geiger.[44] He was a sociologist known only for the meritorious work of his late great friend Paolo Farneti. In the 1950s, Geiger, definitively disproved the objectivist theory of needs and interests typical of orthodox Marxism, based on his research. Workers experience their membership of a trade union one way and their party allegiances in another way. This indicates multiple approaches to workers' actions and their symbolic place in the world. This diversity coexists in a multiple personality.

They live between precarious work, flexibility, undeclared work and even stable, permanent employment.

Workers who do not work in large and medium-sized factories are random and shifting, without group allegiances. At one time, major public industry and major private food industries, for example, laid down the law, fixed the rules and standardised (as far as one can tame free spirits) awareness and behaviour.

Nowadays blue-collar workers are not instantly recognisable from their clothing, as used to be the case, particularly with British manual workers. This came about because such workers earn very different wages and therefore men and women wear very different clothing, picking up what they can from sales, discount stores, retail outlets and market stalls.

The same applied to their diets and leisure time. Manual workers exist by differentiating themselves from other workers and not by uniting, as they used to.

These phenomena are the same all over the world.

It would be a great scientific and moral venture to compare these differences and place them in a meaningful relationship with one another.

We need to remember that studies on work, and more specifically on the working class, have a long tradition.

We need to start from that tradition.

The intellectual work in this area has not flowed continuously but periodically re-emerges like an underground river that first sprung up with the work of Frederick Engels[45] on the working class in Britain at the dawn of Marxism, and which continues to this day without any natural leaders to replace Marx's companion.

The river forked with the birth of modern sociology, based on principles that were already in Engel's work.

Some studied the living conditions of workers in a historical and philosophical context: the specific historical analysis was intended to lay the empirical or meta-empirical grounds to support an eschatological project. This tributary of the river does not interest us here, even though we must bear it in mind conceptually if we are to avoid being caught up in its whirlpools and eddies. In order not to fall into this trap, anyone who wants to make a scientific study of work as it relates to workers must again refer to Theodor Geiger.

Geiger argued that no scientific research can be conducted into workers by embracing an objectivist theory of interests and hence also workers' interests. An objectivist theory presupposes that socially stratified populations (whether organised or not) are historically always led to live out their destinies in accordance with a scatological model even if those populations are unaware of the model. This gives rise to the "general interests of the working class", "class consciousness" and the famous Marxist distinction between "class in itself" and "class for itself" that Lukacs made famous by turning it into a kind of anti-positivist philosophical manifesto.

Marx had seen too many failed revolutions since 1948 and the Paris Commune and knew very well that the "class in itself" sociographic identification of a segment of social stratification based on income and position in the mechanism of capital accumulation was much more congenial to scientific analysis and that "class for itself" was a very rare situation that could assume very different forms and stripes including trade union, mutual, solidarity-based, cooperative and even "revolutionary" associations, the latter being typical of international workers' parties.

Geiger dismantled this entire house of cards through a simple conceptual move: interests exist only in so far as they are recognised by the consciousness of subjects.

This is why we must study *people* in the manner we consider most appropriate to bring out these kinds of consciousness, using the techniques of ethnography and anthropological science rather than psychoanalysis. We are convinced that this method covers a greater range of managerial implications.

We need to act in order to understand what is happening in the heart of modern capitalism in the middle ground between flows of consciousness and the image that we reconstruct of working relations through these flows.

I use the term "working relations" with the emphasis on "relations". We do not want to describe plant layout, machinery configurations, design mechanisms, working rhythms and methods or relationships of authority and ownership, but what all this means for the symbolic world of subjects, that is how they construct (by setting themselves in relation to these social and technical elements) a priority agenda in the way they live their lives and a league table of "cultural preferences" that many trendy analysts referred to as opinions and attitudes.

It goes without saying that we are all dwarves standing on the shoulders of giants, but we should refuse to stand on the shoulders of certain giants.

Firstly, Bravemann[46] and the entire aristocracy of US Marxism gathered around Baran and Sweezy[47] and the "Monthly Review", claimed that workers and clerks (their inspiration was Krakauer in the 1920s) were destined to live in the perennial anarchy of alienation because there is no room for subjective freedom in labour within monopolistic capital.

In the 1980s, I even refused to go along with my fellow dwarves who preached, unlike me, that the advent of the mass worker was the only objectivist fate of labour and therefore talking about symbolic values such as pride in a trade, acceptance of technical authority and worker productiveness was a blasphemy that barred one from the salons of left and right-wing alike: if you talked about labour at all, you had to take the radical chic line and not let on you had studied proper sociology.[48]

This was the same the world over.

For example, in France in the 1960s, Naville and Friedmann[49] predicted the fragmentation of labour as the fragmentation of consciousness.

Only the UK was an oasis of analytical good sense.

During the first half of the 1960s, two great interpreters of the sociology of work, Lockwood and Goldthorpe,[50] gathered a core of academics around themselves and began to work using mixed methods on what Max Weber would have termed the "orientation to action" that workers manifested in their work.

They used mixed techniques, ranging from a sample of scientifically administered questionnaires to guided interviews. They did not use the main working tool (in my opinion) which is the ethnographic and anthropological interview, but their results were methodologically extremely important.

I tried to do something similar on a large scale when I was very young and inexperienced by conducting a survey on behalf of ISVET (*Istituto per gli Studi sullo Sviluppo Economico e il Progresso Tecnico*, Institute for Economic Development and Technical Progress Studies), Eni's research office at that time. The study lasted about six years, from the mid-1970s to the early 1980s, yet it was never published.

I would like to say a few words about the research conducted by Lockwood and Goldthorpe because it will be an essential basis for research projects I hope will come in the future.

They worked on three completely different forms of business: an engine factory working to order with highly skilled workers; a car factory with a mass production line and predominantly unskilled workers; and a service company mainly employing clerks, that is office workers.

The important thing about the research was the conclusions they reached.

While everyone devoured Bravemann avidly, they undermined his presuppositions. Or rather, they interpreted the question of anarchy in a completely different, non-ideological way, which led them to reconstruct the subjective world of workers in accordance with a rising curve of detachment from anomie that peaked with the workers' professional pride in the engines they made. The curve then gradually tailed off in the case of mass production workers, where professional pride was replaced by an orientation to action determined by broader accessibility to the consumer society that the work and its wages made possible.

Hence the seminal position in those books of "workers with an instrumental orientation", who built the agenda of their symbolic and social preferences not based on professional pride but on potential access to the cornucopia of consumption, as if they were continuously living out the final scene of the Michelangelo Antonioni film "Zabriskie Point".

Because the work conducted by these two great British researchers constitutes the pinnacle of scientific thinking on manual workers and clerks, we will use it as our benchmark.

Another father of the great British sociological tradition, Runciman,[51] also emerged in the extraordinary environment of the Labour-oriented Birkbeck College and developed the concept of "reference model" and "relative deprivation".

These concepts also stemmed from the analytical techniques of Lockwood and Goldthorpe and mapped the expectations expressed by specific groups of workers towards consumption patterns.

In this way, they sought to come up with a qualitative measurement of the degree of deprivation, in other words the workers' perceived fall in status due to not achieving those consumption models.

This research by Runciman is also seminal because it allows us to process our view of our own analysis cognitively, bearing in mind the concept of instrumental work as well as that of status, which is crucial for understanding all social relationships. It is crucial and also twofold.

It is comparable to the difference described by Rousseau between *amour de soi* and *amour propre*. The latter is a convention that society imposes on subjects by making them slaves to it. It is therefore a social status that comes from outside the subject. *L'amour de soi* is what an individual thinks of him or herself and it is no coincidence that Rousseau states it to be an essential form of the primitive relationship that *le bon sauvage* puts into action immediately after birth: it is the relationship that establishes the *pitié* or compassion that one person feels for another.

Reconstructing this compassion in society was the unattainable dream of Rousseau, the self-styled Solitary Walker. Given that, unlike Rousseau, we have to walk in society, we will consider both forms of status in an attempt to interpolate symbolic material on relationships of status in work and of work obtained from the interviews with a more general analysis of living communities and personal histories, in other words everything that revolves around an individual in society.

A range of themes amounting to an extraordinary analytical breakthrough emerges even today, though the study observed the reality of work and the researchers spoke familiarly to the workers.

I am convinced of its merit and certain I am not exaggerating or allowing myself to be carried away by the love I have gradually built up for this scientific work, which has always been an extraordinary human experience: "life in relationship", as Simone Weil put it.[52]

The first thing to emerge, apart from local differentiations, is the existence and persistence of a working tradition of life that emanates from the interviewees' households. Workers still have an extraordinary symbolic and anthropological background that is much more fertile than commonly believed. As we travel further south, it is taken over by a peasant past of misery and drudgery, compared to which workers' lives are a universe of emancipation and liberation.

The same can be said about work and the aspiration to work in large as opposed to small and micro-enterprises, as well as the transition from uncertain temporary employment to the secure continuous work offered by big companies.

Big companies symbolically reflect, in the awareness of interview subjects and their stories, a kind of "happy island": this expression crops up frequently because of the connotations of security and general respect emanating from their historical place in their respective proprietary traditions. A significant gap also emerges between academic life and occasional, intermittent apprenticeship, and knowledge intrinsic to a working discipline and the world of work acquired in the relationship with those present in their factory before the newcomers arrived, with their rituals myths and practices. Stories about the way trades are learned are the most diverse and make up a map of feelings and experiences.

There has been a change in the way skills used to be randomly acquired, in other words based on chance meetings with an older person or master craftsman and the much more rationalised current situation (due to the work done by the managerial organisation of processing and manufacture over time to make this process less sporadic and random).

Pride in a trade is very widespread: it transcends differences in age and geographical origin and is the fount of authority in production.

Instrumental attitudes to the task and the job itself are not absent but neither are they prevalent, even in younger generations. Lack of fairness and positive uniformity in incentive and disincentive systems and therefore in the development of this pride is still strongly present and keenly felt by those who expect justice.

Pride in being part of a big company that achieves world-leading levels of technology is also always present among workers, even though their sense of injustice is more keenly felt.

This is perhaps the most important sign of relative deprivation present among the strata of manual workers as well as all employees.

Intergenerational differences are particularly marked with regard to this issue but not as strong as they appear at first sight. In any case, they reveal a situation that is extremely diversified and open to interpretation in the judgements and interpersonal politics that individuals build in their working lives.

Whatever anyone says, technical authority and pride at a good job well done is still the most positive element to emerge from these participatory observations and is an essential aspect of work with the new capitalist machinery.

Disappearance of Trade Unions: Deinstitutionalised Capitalism?

A radical change is under way in the new capitalist machinery, which is commensurate with financialisation and not opposed to mechanisation.

A very dense technocratic and institutional superfetation (in the words of Simmel) or accretion is occurring, particularly in Europe, within the powers that be (prominent examples are the European Monetary Fund, the OECD, European bureaucracies and interstate African and South African bureaucracies). At the same time, we are following the dictates of full-blown liberal capitalism to steadily dismantle institutions of "production and work" typical of the pluralism in industrial relations that the English-speaking school has accustomed us to in order to make them increasingly functional, in the belief that they are a fundamental civilising element of capitalism.

Significantly enough, this crisis has not affected employers' organisations but workers' organisations: workers' trade unions in every latitude and longitude where the new capitalism has made its presence felt.

A serious and critical reflection on workers' trade unions is required, whether association or class-based.

This situation is reminiscent of passage 1.1–45 in John's Gospel, where Martha, sister of Lazarus almost stopped Jesus on the threshold of the tomb, saying that her beloved brother's body had been lying there for four days and was already starting to smell. We know that Jesus did not stop, and Lazarus rose from the dead. We know that the trade unions are not comparable to Lazarus. But this is not the reason why the metaphor is unsound.

Workers' unions certainly risk undergoing a slow and inexorable process of decomposition on a world scale, despite their many differences.

A social body, like a trades union, must perform its intrinsic bodily functions in order to survive and continue to grow.

The essence of a workers' union is a contract between both sides of industry and between both sides of industry and governments. Trade unions continue to perform this function throughout the world under different institutional regimes (unless terrorist dictatorships such as that of the Chinese Communist Party are at work), but almost by inertia, due to organisational loyalty. This should be stopped unless we want to see the emergence of a terrible, uncontrolled micro-conflict and a crisis of anomie that could threaten the productive and reproductive continuity of society as a whole.

This task is becoming increasingly difficult.

The new capitalism we have described here has triggered a long decline in workers' trade unions.

A slow deconstruction of industrial relations in the hands and minds of the state rather than in the hands and minds of both sides of industry—employers' and workers' organisations—has paradoxically led to this completely new global situation and is one cause of the colossal transfer of wealth from labour to capital that has occurred throughout the world in recent years.

Over-legislation of industrial relations has changed them from social relationships into paragovernmental relationships and done away with their original historical function, which lies in both conflict and building relationships and agreements between the sides.

This does not mean that the state must be expunged from industrial relationships formed in society, but it must serve them and not rule them.

The tradition of trade union pluralism is certainly different from the class-based tradition of Lassalle.

Trade union policy lines derived from these two different approaches have turned out to be incompatible in the long term.

For example, both lines of action are clearly highlighted in the case of the increasingly crucial struggle against inequality, whatever philosophical and economic concepts each of us is free to pursue.

Those in the grip of a parastatal approach will focus mainly on tax leverage to reduce inequalities in the mistaken illusion that in the long run any aggregate demand that may arise will act as a multiplier of growth and therefore employment. In nations and economic areas with long periods of low growth and enormous destruction of effective aggregate demand (affecting companies), this approach has little effect on employment or productive growth. At best, it can feebly counter the deflationist trends going on all over the world.

A completely different scenario can be created by a trade union playing a prominent role in the social construction of a system of industrial relations that hinges on the relationship between both sides of industry rather than statism.

In this case, the link is not the relationship with public finance but with the ability of the trade union and others to promote an increase in production capacity, labour productivity and the wage bill.

In this case, the first outcome may promote an increase in investment (because investment makes profit and not vice versa) with a consequent increase in employment.

If we consider that all future predictions about a company's systemic configuration hinge on innovations that save labour but increase production capacity and competition and thus make room for trade union bargaining to convert constant capital into variable capital and variable capital into wages, it is easy to understand that this should be the challenge thrown down to trade union organisations worldwide.

This is all the more true because savings on the public finance bill and therefore public expenditure that can be achieved in this way can also lead to an increase in income from work given the huge number of jobs that are bound to be created in the corporate and personal service sectors and particularly the personal care sector. This applies to the entire set of jobs and activities that will have an impact on generations of workers and retired people (the elderly), laying the foundations for a new quality of social reproduction and hence quality of life.

This could also result in a reform in welfare, changing it from state-based only to a solidarity-based organisation founded on the community.

Reproduction of society is becoming ever more central to the new international capital structure, particularly in nations with well-established industrialisation and a mature advanced service structure.

Technological change and the ongoing cyclical nature of a financial structure that increasingly rules capitalist profit generates a kind of social fragmentation that faces the state with new and immense tasks from the viewpoint of old forms of social protection, welfare, preservation of complex natural societies, kinship and families, who find themselves having to shoulder tasks forced on them by the state fiscal crisis.

Only the rebirth of community as a system of relationships and values—often supporting and not taking precedence over trade values—will allow the reproduction of societies that are increasingly less based on the productive mechanism of creating capitalist profit alone. Such societies will depend more on the unpaid work of networks of friends and natural or social relatives—communities in other words—that allow the same economic growth or dispel the stress of negative growth by recession and deflation, as happens now in capitalist cycles.

Where economic growth happens without these social networks of reproduction, we see emerging crises of employment and consumption, coupled with anarchy anomie and an absence of recognition and relationships.

The less fairness there is, the more difficult it becomes to generate sustainable social reproduction that is not killed off by the blows of inequality and anomie, fostering the genuine human despair that we also sadly see around us.

The quest for mutuality therefore becomes a need for community relationships and support in the ideal city state.

All forms of community and cooperation must be supported, helped, encouraged and developed by human behaviour and not by artificial means that again destroy community and mutuality with the state-centred, kleptocratic support of small groups.

This new welfare is also affecting the system of industrial relations with increasing force, spreading a message that was once exclusive to the English-speaking trade unions, from Australia to the US, with their mutualistic and neo-associative tradition of tackling thorny welfare reform issues.

This is a new frontier of trade unionism—now called upon to question its nature and role in strengthening its strategic position in the society it is called upon to change—and also of cooperation, particularly with regard to old people affected by unfair policies and growing economic and social inequality. Trade unions must now forge a new path and generate new hope.

Notes

1. The best example of this theoretical froth, which has passed into popular belief with consequences similar to those wreaked by a weapon of mass destruction (cognitive and behavioural), can be seen in M. Jensen and W. Meckling, *Theory of the Firm: Managerial Behavior, Agency Cost and Ownership Structure*, in "Journal of Financial Economics", Issue 3, 1976.
2. Note. Kondratiev, "*Die langen* Sozialwissenschaft und Sozialpolitik" 56: 573–609, 1926, returned to in Review of Economic Statistics (1935) and again in "*The Long Waves in Economic Life*." Review of Economic Statistics 17 (6): 105–115. 1935. After he was shot and killed during the purges of 1938, his main works were collected in *Dynamics of Economic Development: Long Cycles and Industrial Growth in Historical Context*. London: Macmillan, 1998.
3. A. Gerschenkron, *Economic Backwardness in Historical Perspective*, Harvard University Press, Cambridge, MA, 1962.
4. M. King, *The End of Alchemy: Money, Banking, and the Future of the Global Economy*, Norman and Company, New York, 2016.
5. See the very fine work by T. F. Gelthner, *Stress Test: Reflections on Financial Crisis*, The Business Book, London, 2014.
6. See the interesting comparison in M. K. Brunnemeier, H, James, J. Landau, *The Euro and the Battles of Ideas*, Princeton University Press, Princeton and Oxford, 2016.
7. P. Sraffa, *Production of Commodities by means of Commodities. Prelude to a Critique of Economic Theory*, Cambridge University Press, Cambridge, 1960.
8. E. Rullani, *Lavoro in transizione: prove di quarta rivoluzione industriale in Italia*, due for publication.
9. H. Kern, M. Schuman, *Das Ende der Arbeiststeilung? Rationalisierung in der Industriellen Produktion*, Verlag Bech'sche, Munchen, 1984.

10. See also my own *Organizzazione, lavoro e innovazione industriale nell' Italia tra le due guerre*, Rosenberg and Sellier, Turin, 1978.
11. Note Kondratieff, *op. cit.*
12. The reference is to P. Marsh, *The New Industrial Revolution*, Yale University Press, New Haven, 2012.
13. E. Brynjolfsson and A. McAfee, *The Second Machine Age: Work, Progress and Prosperity in a Time of Brilliant Technologies*, Norton, 2014. *La tecnologia aiuta il lavoro?* with my *Presentazione*, Go Ware, Firenze, 2014. Si vedano anche: T. Cowen, *Is Over: Powering America beyond the Age of the Great Stagnation*, Plume, 2014. For an illuminating discussion on these topics, see *The Robots Are Coming* by J. Lanchester, in "London Review of Books", Vol. 37, No. 5, 5 March 2015, pages 3–8.
14. E. Brynjolfsson and A. McAfee, *cit.*
15. T. Cowen, *cit.*
16. R. Solow, *Growth theory: an exposition*, Oxford, Clarendon Press, 1970.
17. R. J. Gordon, *Is U.S. Economic Growth Over? Faltering Innovation Confronts the Six Headwinds*, NBER Working Paper No. 18315, August 2012.
18. The unmistakable reference is to Volume 5 of the work by *J. Maynard Keynes, The General Theory of Employment, Interest and Money*, Londra, Macmillan, 1936.
19. C. Benedykt Frey et M. A. Osborne *The future of employment: How susceptible are jobs to computerisation?* WHO Working Paper, Oxford, September 2013.
20. A. Hansen, *Full Recovery or Stagnation*, Norton Company, New York, 1938.
21. J. Lanchester, *The Robots Are Coming, cit.*
22. M. Ford, *Rise of the Robot. Technology and the Threat of a Jobless Future*, Basic Books, New York, 2014.
23. J. A. Schumpeter, *The theory of economic development: an inquiry into profits, capital, credit, interest, and the business cycle*. Transaction Books, New Brunswick–New Jersey, 1934–1983.
24. M. Ford, *cit*, p. 123.
25. G. Sapelli, *Organizzazione, lavoro e innovazione industriale nell' Italia tra le due guerre*, Rosenberg and Sellier, Turin, 1978, G. Sapelli, *Economia, tecnologia e direzione d' impresa in Italia*, Einaudi, Turin, 1994.
26. M. Granovetter, *The Impact of Social Structure on Economic Outcomes*, in "Journal of Economic Perspectives", vol. 19, n. 1, 2005, pp. 33–50, M. Magatti, *Il potere istituente della società civile*, Laterza, Bari, 2005.

27. P. Alferj, A. Favazzo, *La manifattura additiva. Una grande opportunità*, in "Impresa e città", n. 1, 2015, pp. 17–30. I must also quote (Centro Studi Confindustria), *La manifattura additiva. Alcune valutazioni economiche con particolare riferimento all' industria italiana*, in "Scenari industriale", n. 5, 2014, pp. 1–23.
28. A. Granelli, L. De Biase, *Inventori d' Italia*, Guerini & Associati, Milan, 2014.
29. N. Rosenberg, *Inside the Black Box: Technology and Economics*, Cambridge University Press, Cambridge, MA, 1983.
30. Alfred Marshall, *Elements of economics of industry, London, Macmillan, 1892 and interesting reflections on the topic*, in J. K. Whitaker (ed.) *Centenary Essays on Alfred Marshall*, Cambridge University Press, 1990.
31. T. Khun, *The Structure of Scientific Revolutions*, Chicago University Press, Chicago, 1962.
32. J. P. Kruth, M. C. Leu, T. Nakagawa, Progress in Additive Manufacturing and Rapid Prototyping, "Annals of the CIRP", vol. 47/2/1998, pp. 525–540.
33. A fantastic description of the history of these processes is given in a work by various authors entitled *Metal Fabrication by Additive Manufacturing Using Laser and Electron Beam Melting Technologies*, in "JMST", 2012, 28(1), pp. 1–14.
34. B. Baufeld, O. Van der Biest, R. Gaut, *Additive manufacturing of Ti-6Al-4V components by shaped metal deposition: Microstructure and Mechanical properties*, in "Materials and Design", 31(20101), pp. 5106–5111.
35. A. A. V. V., Three-dimensional Printing: The Physic and implications of Additive Manufacturing, in "CIRP Annals. Manufacturing Technology", vol. 42, issue 1, 1993, pp. 257–280.
36. G. N. Levy, *The role and future of the Laser Technology in the Additive Manufacturing environment*, in "Physic Procedia" Key Note Paper, 2010.
37. S. Mellor, L. Hao, D. Zhang, *Additive Manufacturing frame work for implementation*, in "International Journal of Production Economics", 149, (2014), pp. 194–201.
38. Op. *cit.*, p. 195.
39. Op. *cit.*, p. 196.
40. G. Sapelli, *Per una cultura dell' impresa. Strategia e saper del management moderno*, Franco Angeli/ISVET, Milan, 1989.
41. E. PUGLIESE (edited by), *L'inchiesta sociale in Italia*, Carocci, Rome, 2008.

42. For an overview of the practice of conducting interviews in order to study corporate history, see. D. BIGAZZI, *Impresa, lavoro e fabbrica: alcune riflessioni sull'utilizzo delle testimonianze orali*, in R. COVINO (edited by), *Fonti orali e storia dell'impresa. Atti del seminario nazionale di Arezzo, 15 ottobre 1993*, Rubbettino, Soveria Mannelli 2000, pp. 39–53; our methodological principles differ, but see in particular M. S. FISHER, G. DAWNEY (edited by), *Frontiers of Capital. Ethnographic Reflections on the New Economy*, Duke University Press, Durham-London, 2006.
43. W. Sombart, *Warum gibt es in den Vereinigten Staaten keinen Sozialismus?* Tübingen: Mohr, 1906.
44. T. Geiger, Demokratie ohne Dogma: Die Gesellschaft zwischen Pathos und Nüchternheit. Munich: Szczesny, 1963 and a work by P. Farneti, *Theodor Geiger e la coscienza della società industriale*, Turin, Giappichelli, 1966.
45. F. Engels, *Die Lage der arbeitenden Klasse in England, Lipsia, 1845.*
46. H. Braveman, *Labor and Monopoly Capital. The Degradation of Work in the Twentieth Century*, Monthly Review Press, New York, 1974.
47. P. Baran & M. Sweezy, *Monopoly Capital: An Essay on the American Economy and Social Order*, Monthly Review Press, New York, 1966.
48. G. Sapelli, *La cultura della produzione:"autorità tecnica e "autonomia morale*", in (edited by B. Bottiglieri and P. Celli), "Le culture del lavoro e l' esperienza di Torino nel quadro europeo", Il Mulino, Bologna, 1987, pp. 23–52 and pp. 157–160 (*Una replica*).
49. G. Freidmann et P. Naville, *Traité de scociologie du travail*, Editions Armand Colin, Paris, 1961.
50. J.H. Goldthorpe and D.W. Lockwood, F. Bechlofer, J. Platt, *The Affluent Worker: Industrial Attitudes and Behavior*, Cambridge University Press, Cambridge, 1969.
51. G. Runcuiman, *Relative Deprivation and Social Justice*, Penguin Books, London, 1972.
52. S. Weil, *La condition ouvriére*, Gallimard, Paris, 1951.

Bibliography

M. Jensen and W. Meckling, *Theory of the Firm: Managerial Behavior, Agency Cost and Ownership Structure*, in "Journal of Financial Economics", Issue 3, 1976.

Kondratiev, "*Die langen* Sozialwissenschaft und Sozialpolitik" 56: 573–609, 1926, returned to in Review of Economic Statistics (1935) and again in "*The Long Waves in Economic Life.*" Review of Economic Statistics 17 (6): 105–115. 1935. After he was shot and killed during the purges of 1938, his main works were collected in *Dynamics of Economic Development: Long Cycles and Industrial Growth in Historical Context*. London: Macmillan, 1998.

A. Gerschenkron, *Economic Backwardness in Historical Perspective*, Harvard University Press, Cambridge, MA, 1962.

M. King, The End of Alchemy: Money, Banking, and the Future of the Global Economy, Norman and Company, New York, 2016.

T. F. Gelthner, *Stress Test: Reflections on Financial Crisis*, The Business Book, London, 2014.

M. K. Brunnemeier, H, James, J. Landau, *The Euro and the Battles of Ideas*, Princeton University Press, Princeton and Oxford, 2016.

P. Sraffa, *Production of Commodities by means of Commodities. Prelude to a Critique of Economic Theory*, Cambridge University Press, Cambridge, 1960.

E. Rullani, *Lavoro in transizione: prove di quarta rivoluzione industriale in Italia*, due for publication.

H. Kern, M. Schuman, *Das Ende der Arbeiststeilung? Rationalisierung in der Industriellen Produktion*, Verlag Bech'sche, Munchen, 1984.

See also my own *Organizzazione, lavoro e innovazione industriale nell' Italia tra le due guerre*, Rosenberg and Sellier, Turin, 1978.

Note Kondratieff, *op. cit.*

P. Marsh, *The New Industrial Revolution*, Yale University Press, New Haven, 2012.

E. Brynjolfsson and A. McAfee, *The Second Machine Age: Work, Progress and Prosperity in a Time of Brilliant Technologies*, Norton, 2014. *La tecnologia aiuta il lavoro?* with my *Presentazione*, Go Ware, Firenze, 2014.

T. Cowen, *Is Over: Powering America beyond the Age of the Great Stagnation*, Plume, 2014.

The Robots Are Coming by J. Lanchester, in "London Review of Books", Vol. 37, No. 5, 5 March 2015, pages 3–8.

R. Solow, *Growth theory: an exposition*, Oxford, Clarendon Press, 1970.

R. J. Gordon, *Is U.S. Economic Growth Over? Faltering Innovation Confronts the Six Headwinds*, NBER Working Paper No. 18315, August 2012.

J. Maynard Keynes, The General Theory of Employment, Interest and Money, London, Macmillan, 1936.

C. Benedykt Frey and M. A. Osborne *The future of employment: How susceptible are jobs to computerisation?* WHO Working Paper, Oxford, September 2013.

A. Hansen, *Full Recovery or Stagnation*, Norton Company, New York, 1938.
M. Ford, *Rise of the Robot. Technology and the Threat of a Jobless Future*, Basic Books, New York, 2014.
J. A. Schumpeter, *The theory of economic development: an inquiry into profits, capital, credit, interest, and the business cycle*. Transaction Books, New Brunswick- New Jersey, 1934–1983.
G. Sapelli, *Organizzazione, lavoro e innovazione industriale nell' Italia tra le due guerre*, Rosenberg and Sellier, Turin, 1978.
G. Sapelli, *Economia, tecnologia e direzione d' impresa in Italia*, Einaudi, Turin, 1994.
M. Granovetter, *The Impact of Social Structure on Economic Outcomes*, in "Journal of Economic Perspectives", vol. 19, n. 1, 2005, pp. 33–50.
M. Magatti, *Il potere istituente della società civile*, Laterza, Bari, 2005.
P. Alferj, A. Favazzo, *La manifattura additiva. Una grande opportunità*, in "Impresa e città", n. 1, 2015, pp. 17–30.
Centro Studi Confindustria, *La manifattura additiva. Alcune valutazioni economiche con particolare riferimento all' industria italiana*, in "Scenari industriali", n. 5, 2014, pp. 1–23.
A. Granelli, L. De Biase, *Inventori d' Italia*, Guerini & Associati, Milan, 2014.
N. Rosenberg, *Inside the Black Box: Technology and Economics*, Cambridge University Press, Cambridge, MA, 1983.
Alfred Marshall, Elements of economics of industry, *London, Macmillan, 1892 and interesting reflections on the topic*, in J. K. Whitaker (ed.) *Centenary Essays on Alfred Marshall*, Cambridge University Press, 1990.
T. Khun, *The Structure of Scientific Revolutions*, Chicago University Press, Chicago, 1962.
J. P. Kruth, M.C. Leu, T. Nakagawa, *Progress in Additive Manufacturing and Rapid Prototyping*, "Annals of the CIRP", vol. 47/2/1998, pp. 525–540.
Metal Fabrication by Additive Manufacturing Using Laser and Electron Beam Melting Technologies, in "JMST", 2012, 28(1), pp. 1–14.
B. Baufeld, O. Van der Biest, R. Gaut, *Additive manufacturing of Ti-6Al-4V components by shaped metal deposition: Microstructure and Mechanical properties*, in "Materials and Design", 31 (2010), pp. 5106–5111.
A. A. V. V., Three-dimensional Printing: The Physic and implications of Additive Manufacturing, in "CIRP Annals. Manufacturing Technology", vol. 42, issue 1, 1993, pp. 257–280.
G. N. Levy, *The role and future of the Laser Technology in the Additive Manufacturing environment*, in "Physic Procedia" Key Note Paper, 2010.

S. Mellor, L. Hao, D. Zhang, *Additive Manufacturing frame work for implementation*, in "International Journal of Production Economics", 149, (2014), pp. 194–201.

G. Sapelli, *Per una cultura dell'impresa. Strategia e saper del management moderno*, Franco Angeli/ISVET, Milan, 1989.

E. Pugliese (ed.), *L'inchiesta sociale in Italia*, Carocci, Rome, 2008.

D. Bigazzi, *Impresa, lavoro e fabbrica: alcune riflessioni sull'utilizzo delle testimonianze orali*, in R. COVINO (ed.), *Fonti orali e storia dell'impresa. Atti del seminario nazionale di Arezzo, 15 ottobre 1993*, Rubbettino, Soveria Mannelli 2000, pp. 39–53; our methodological principles differ, but see in particular M.S. Fisher, G. Dawney (ed.), *Frontiers of Capital. Ethnographic Reflections on the New Economy*, Duke University Press, Durham–London, 2006.

W. Sombart, *Warum gibt es in den Vereinigten Staaten keinen Sozialismus?* Tübingen: Mohr, 1906.

T. Geiger, Demokratie ohne Dogma: Die Gesellschaft zwischen Pathos und Nüchternheit. Munich: Szczesny, 1963.

P. Farneti, *Theodor Geiger e la coscienza della società industriale*, Turin, Giappichelli, 1966.

F. Engels, *Die Lage der arbeitenden Klasse in England, Lipsia,* 1845.

H. Braveman, *Labor and Monopoly Capital. The Degradation of Work in the Twentieth Century*, Monthly Review Press, New York, 1974.

P. Baran & M. Sweezy, *Monopoly Capital: An Essay on the American Economy and Social Order*, Monthly Review Press, New York, 1966.

G. Sapelli, *La cultura della produzione:"autorità tecnica e "autonomia morale"*, in (edited by B. Bottiglieri and P. Celli), "Le culture del lavoro e l' esperienza di Torino nel quadro europeo", Il Mulino, Bologna, 1987, pp. 23–52 and pp. 157–160.

G. Freidmann and P. Naville, *Traité de scociologie du travail*, Editions Armand Colin, Paris, 1961.

J. H. Goldthorpe and D.W. Lockwood, F. Bechlofer, J. Platt, *The Affluent Worker: Industrial Attitudes and Behavior*, Cambridge University Press, Cambridge, 1969.

G. Runcuiman, *Relative Deprivation and Social Justice*, Penguin Books, London, 1972.

S. Weil, *La condition ouvrière*, Gallimard, Paris, 1951.

3

Is a Non-capitalist Economy Possible?

Histories, Wars, Markets

The general message we can take from the previous sections about this specific juncture in human history is that we cannot resign ourselves to a future determined by absence of work and growing inequality.

This is what we learn from the "world of capitalist machines".

Yet another message also emerges from the same world, underpinning the process of capital appreciation: the manner of allocating fully capitalist property rights rather than the technological process itself causes the collapse of employment.

The capacity for human intelligence emanating from this process is immense and we must seek a type of socioeconomic system that is not affected by the immense contradiction between relationships of production and technological processing.

We must address the problem of creating another type of production relationship and look for a potential range of production and property relationships.

This goes totally against the prevailing *zeitgeist*.

G. Sapelli, *Beyond Capitalism*, https://doi.org/10.1007/978-3-030-20769-4_3

Another of the ideological ideas that has now become commonplace and generally accepted is the assumption that the prevailing socioeconomic system will always be capitalist.

Anyone who has studied the classics knows that this is not at all likely.

The proof lies in the long-term coexistence, alongside gradually rolled-out types of capitalism, of forms of economic relations that are not overdetermined by private property and the expropriation of work surplus and its conversion to surplus value and capitalist profit.

When capitalism was in its infancy, which paradoxically happened on a national scale and was unaffected by the disintermediation of production and social reproduction, the interdependence of global trade spread and the rules of capitalist exchange and appreciation had a distinctly international flavour.

Up to World War I, these rules ensured a degree of economic independence even higher than at present, under the unchallenged rule of the UK. This nation "ruled the waves" and, after mastering technological development together with Germany, it then went on to conquer Asia and Africa.

The end of World War I in the twentieth century had two effects.

The first was to plunge the world and its economy into a conglomeration of economic nationalisms. These included all forms of "communism", which rose up with the collapse of empires, particularly the czarist empire.

The second effect was to prevent full global deployment of North American rule at a time when the US was set to take over domination of the oceans and skies, advocating free-market principles, because its military power was infinitely greater than that of the UK.

World War II and then the Cold War prevented this dominion from expanding peacefully.

The collapse of the USSR then came about due to a set of disruptive military and economic forces.

Economic interdependency again came into play and led to the type of globalisation we are experiencing today.

Nowadays it is obvious to everyone that the market is an artificial construct: it is the result of a set of rules that humans and their associations are able to build.

The sovereign's sword was able to stop warfare at fairs in the Middle Ages: without it, there could be no market and no traders.

Market regulation institutions now perform the same role: they impose a separation between warfare and markets by reducing bankruptcies and erecting barriers to entry, making it more or less complicated for new members to gain access to the fair, which is now predominantly financial. There are no more physical commodity exchanges in the world, not even in Chicago (which was the commodity exchange *par excellence* for centuries). They have all been dematerialised with transaction costs tending to zero through the use of ICT.

The risk of accountability failing is very high if one operates in an unregulated system, as happened after the collapse of the USSR through the joint action of the US Democrats and the European socialists driven by the hegemonic cultural force of the global financial powers.

They dismantled the rules introduced by Roosevelt (the Glass Steel Act, separating commercial banks from business banks, is the best-known) protecting the market against excess risk: everything is ethically corrupted and sinking into crisis due to surplus production capacity and too much of the very-high-risk financialisation in which we are immersed these days.

This must be the starting point of every economic and political debate.

To buck the trend, we must make stable savings and full employment central to our thinking. It would be a mistake—and this is my core message—to respond to market failures by invoking a new form of statism or a new form of global protectionism.

Growth would grind to a halt to an even great extent than it has already. We would enter a deep recession or stagnation similar to that experienced by Japan in the 1990s and Germany a few years later.

We need to rediscover the principles of market subsidiarity.

In other words, the only way out of today's capitalist crisis is to implement a thrifty, light-handed process of cultural change to encourage market actors to self-regulate and not build heavy-handed state control systems.

Subsidiarity must perform the role of self-regulation and act as a guiding compass. This also applies to its place in the market, to quote the Grand Inquisitors of the twentieth century.

Fairness, simple rules and compliance, which are not state-regulated but left up to the moral rules of stakeholders, must be the order of the day.

Above all, personal communication and transparency must overcome the fetishism of commodities. Capitalism is a set of personal relationships, even though they look to us like relationships between commodities. This is because the power of the financial and proprietorial classes overturns any sense of an economic process and reduces it to the maximisation of capitalist profit, blocking any non-hierarchical free communication between stakeholders.

The revolutionary solution to this is to revive the philosophy and practice of "common goods"—more simply known as the "commons"—on a large scale.

There is a theoretical basis for this. Evidence comes in the form of North American fervour and, earlier still, between the two world wars in Europe, the flourishing of French Catholic personalism[1] and the thoughts of Romano Guardini on Christian personalism (in his unfinished work[2]).

This analytical strand harbours the glimmering of a possible alternative to contemporary capitalism, starting from the assumption that capitalism is not the only way to allocate property rights.

The Problem Is Ownership and Its Variable Forms

> The non-human means of production may be appropriated by workers as individuals or by corporate groups [...]. When appropriated by workers, an individual worker can become the owner of a non-human means of production, or the appropriation may be carried out by a more or less completely closed group of workers. In the latter case, the corporate group is the owner, not the individual worker. Such a corporate group may carry out its functions as a unitary economy, as on a communistic basis, or with appropriation of shares (i.e. on a cooperative basis) [...] as is characteristic of producers' cooperatives.[3]

Max Weber's brilliant definition of cooperative association has long been neglected because it was dismissed as unsound by reductionist economic thinking and then by a sterile debate on the maximisation of income by members and the consequence that this presumed basic notion of cooperative enterprise would have on the behaviour of the enterprise and its cooperative members.

Any political plan to overcome capitalism must begin by rethinking the foundations of cooperative enterprise theory.

A very recent work by a US academic[4] on the optimum theory for allocating the property rights of all enterprises—whether cooperative or not, which is the true distinguishing mark of a cooperative enterprise—has restored the cooperative ideal to the place it deserves in theory and practice.

> An analysis of the performance and role of associative forms, cooperatives, foundations and non-profit organisations provides—states Hansmann—a useful means of measuring the managerial efficiency of traditional capital firms and deepens our understanding of the ways in which and to what ends product markets and capital markets, including those of company control, are used to monitor that efficiency.[5]

We must consider the two significant terms in these quotations in order to talk about the distinctive nature of a cooperative enterprise. Both provide us with the key to understanding the constituent nature of the company. For a company to come about, a collective social action must be established based on a subjective recognition of interests by a group of people. This recognition can only take place through solidarity-based systems (religious, political and civil): Geiger[6] teaches us that an objectivist theory of social interests cannot exist. A cooperative enterprise comes about when this recognition is sparked and begins to operate with the aim of acquiring certain commodities within a market and monetary economy that could not be acquired individually and separately or that would have to be acquired at costs much higher than those that could be achieved through a collective group approach: labour, consumption, credit, housing, personal care, the possibility of creating art not determined by the dictates of the market—or educating and being educated. These are the impetuses that bring about a voluntary action to create an economic association with a social purpose that is different, for example, from a trade union association set up with the aim of acquiring commodities that could not otherwise be acquired through the markets: wages, work and certain social rights.

This is transitory: the action created is transitory (but not the organisation that can stem from it). Striking, for example, never gives rise to an economic association resembling a firm that wishes to operate permanently on the market and attain those assets, not by disrupting the social peace but by working alongside other non-cooperative enterprises.[7]

Hence, the importance of an interpretive model that offers us the second of the above options.

In its most mature form, a cooperative enterprise is an alternative to trade union action and the attendant disruption of social peace. Much has been made of the fact that at the dawn of the cooperative movement, trade union resistance and cooperative action seemed to be phenomena that interacted with one another and were simultaneously present.[8]

Workers' trade unions and cooperation are both outcomes of capitalist development and never arise separately on the world stage. This is the crux of the matter.

When we think back to the origins of the International Cooperative Alliance (ICA), founded in 1895, we immediately appreciate that this sprung from the new British and European or continental capitalist organisations. The international association was clearly based on the need to set itself apart from the international trade union movement, when the cooperative movement began to take its first independent steps in the national and international arena.[9] This need to distinguish itself went hand in hand with the great debates affecting national delegations present at Alliance congresses, which between the nineteenth and twentieth centuries always concerned the definition of cooperation based on its form of ownership. Conflict arose within the British cooperative movement and concerned the tension between producer cooperation and consumer production. The British Vansittart Neale, a Christian socialist, was a fervent advocate of the principle that the workers should wholly own the means of production that they were called upon to manage, by virtue of their educational background. By allocating profits, reserving profit shares for the enterprise to guarantee intergenerational reproduction (the indivisible profit must be kept as a collective group asset), cooperative collective enterprises could gradually proliferate and spread to overcome forms of capitalist production, foreshadowing a kind of "market socialism", which many economists have recently stumbled upon as though it was their own brilliant theoretical invention.[10] The arguments were directed against the very powerful British consumer cooperatives.[11] How can this be? Were they not the cradle of the cooperative movement? In 1845, in Rochdale, the "honest pioneers" had founded the first consumer cooperative which, after Robert Owen's Associations of All Class of All Nations set up in 1835, represented the symbolic early template for the international cooperative movement.

British proponents of producers' cooperatives pointed out two weaknesses in consumer cooperatives with regard to the principles of all-round cooperation, or a form of mutualism that may or may not have been prevalently based on solidarity—in other words, the form of mutualism that is expressed where members' rights become selfish and self-referential. The first weakness was to maximise the advantages of members who acquired assets based on a "closed-door principle", that is not allowing others access to the sales counters. The second weakness—perhaps the most serious and still very active in the global consumer cooperative movement, with the exception of the closed-door system operated by many developing countries—was to treat workers involved in producing the items on sale (which the cooperative produced themselves) and distribution workers as mere employees and proletarians as with any other capitalist enterprise, not allowing them to become members. This happened even years after founding the first consumer cooperative, when the "open door" principle was practised, allowing any member of the public to obtain supplies from cooperatives.

If you read the proceedings of the first Italian Cooperative Alliance (ICA) Congress, you will soon realise that the concept of co-operative theory had yet to be constructed. Very different stances and practices had to be incorporated. The proponents ranged from people who supported Mazzini's principle of profit-sharing in a union of capital and labour, to those who supported cooperation only between smallholders, in the belief that private ownership had to remain the fundamental principle of cooperation and should be diluted to collective ownership only in second-level cooperation (a form of cooperation that united owners' cooperatives by combining them in accordance with typical types of agricultural production). This was evident in Austrian and German versions of the cooperative movement in the agricultural and credit sector.[12]

The practice of association was far ahead of the theory: the ICA was set up and operated consistently, albeit amidst endless theoretical debate and philosophical dissent. In a collection of essays published in Paris in 1912, Tougan Baranosvsky, one of the most important Marxist economists, stressed that no theory of cooperation yet existed and sought one in cooperative profit and the indivisibility inherent in the proprietary form of the enterprise. Charles Gide, a leading light of the French and international cooperative movement at the beginning of the twentieth century, also believed that the essence of cooperation was the mutual bond that shaped a new form of ownership and everything had to follow on from this.

The reason for the essential nature of the discussion about forms of ownership was finally made clear to us when Hansmann fought off differences of opinion and criticisms of his theory in order to pinpoint the essential element establishing the rational allocation of a proprietary resource in accordance with cooperative principles. This becomes clear when we compare forms of an enterprise according to their company titles. This proves that the stress I have always placed[13] on the founding nature of the collective acquisition of a group of commodities that would otherwise be unattainable individually can also be theoretically justified by economic science. The most effective system of ownership is one that guarantees a company a greater cost reduction than it generates through trading. And it operates on the market as well as through its mechanisms of governance. Both performance costs must be considered. The market costs derive from transactions in market-facing commodities or that can be sought in the market for production; business governance costs are derived from control over the organisation's stakeholders-managers exercised by the shareholders as well as management costs inherent in the specific form of ownership adopted. The costs are incurred to minimise market and governance imperfections. The most suitable forms of ownership for companies are therefore those for which the costs of market imperfections are harsher and more burdensome, and which therefore tend to fall steadily despite a loss of effectiveness and efficiency. Prominent among the forms of cost reduction mentioned above are those that operate in accordance with appropriate forms of control over stakeholders responsible for controlling the company, minimising market imperfections:

> The analysis suggests that—states Hansmann—all else being equal, costs will be minimised if ownership is assigned to the class of owners for whom market bargaining problems, in other words the costs of market imperfections, are harsh. For example, if a company holds a natural monopoly in relation to its customers but obtains the capital factor, the labour factor and other production factors from reasonably competitive markets, then the total cost will probably be minimised, assigning ownership to the company's own customers. This helps explain why so many rural electricity production companies are organised as consumer cooperatives.[14]

Hansmann's theory definitely has its limits. The main thing is that it is not a dynamic theory; it is still over-dependent on Marshall-style models of balance, and thus overlooks the fact that businesses are living organisms, and they are associations of people even when they are capitalist or state enterprises. They depend on the market in different ways and to different extents. They are as different as the different institutional market structures and their very diverse company backgrounds. They change in a constant quest to increase the efficiency of their internal mechanisms and the allocation of their ownership rights. If they fail to do this, as often happens, they sink into entropy and ungovernability. This situation of limited rationalism is typical of the deaths of enterprises in Marshall's forests or Durkheim's divisions of social labour.

However, all this has led us to the crux of the matter, which is that of ownership structures placed in the definitive guise of a cooperative enterprise, that is within the context of social division of labour. This belief is common to a large portion of international cooperative thinking, which, despite common belief, continues throughout the world, albeit not with the same vigour as between the nineteenth and twentieth centuries.

One of many examples can be found in the world of Canadian cooperation. In this case, due to the work of Francois Albert Angers, the general consensus is that we need to focus mainly on the distinctive features of cooperative action in relation to the action of populations organised in accordance with capitalist systems or state systems. "These different distinguishing traits reveal—states Angers—that the cooperative movement is by its very nature an economic organisation, in other words organised in accordance with the principle of production in order to satisfy needs".[15] And he continues: "The great fundamental distinction on which everything else depends, between cooperatives, private enterprises and state enterprises, is the nature of the model of 'propriétaire-usager' (which can be translated as 'property that is used' or as 'property of users') on which the cooperative alone builds the practical and ultimately the legal basis of its entire organisational configuration."[16]

The same sentiments are expressed by the leading lights of global neo-reformist research in the UK, where a quest for a new path to equality and non-state-centred socialism has come up with very encouraging results for those who wish to reflect on the possible future.

Charles Leadbeater and Ian Christie have made a major contribution to this field and I will return to this shortly.[17] Firstly, we need to add some background.

It is a significant feature of the new political and cultural context to the contemporary global debate on equality and justice that the universe of cooperation is no longer seen as separate from the universe of mutualism and trade unionism, but as one aspect of the persistence and resurrection of global mutualism. The most keenly felt cooperative thought arose out of a desire to distance itself from the trade union and mutualist experience and even forms of ownership that were worker-based—or solidarity-based if you prefer—in order to affirm its characteristic of being a specific and supportive enterprise that is still founded on cooperative profit and therefore surplus.

The fact that the mutualistic movement is now making a big comeback is a clear sign that the principle of subsidiarity is returning in force. It is making a stand against the spread of liberalism as the only model—for the organisation of society as opposed to the economy—extending beyond the confines of nineteenth- and twentieth-century Catholic social doctrine to become the most important civilising, self-regulatory, anti-statist principle for our future.

Leadbeater and Christie[18] give us the inspiration to address the theoretical heart of this discourse. This is their definition of a "mutual":

> Mutual organisations take many forms, from cooperative to trade unions, building societies and employee-owned businesses. A mutual is organised to serve its members, whether they are consumers (as in mutual insurance), employees (as in worked owned companies) or suppliers (for example in some agricultural co-operatives). Mutuals are organised for and often by their members, who band together with the common purpose of providing a shared service from which they all benefit. Their main competitors are traditional companies, which are run by managers who are ultimately accountable to shareholders, and public sector organisations, which are run by civil servants, overseen by politicians and financed by taxpayers. Our research shows the spirit of mutual aid and co-operatives enterprise is alive.... Mutuals—when they are well run, when they serve appropriate markets and when they are organised on the right scale ... have a significant advantage over the private and public sector organisations with which they compete. This report argues that mutuals can do more than survive; they can thrive in the twenty-first century *service economy* (my italics), because at their best they can harness two ingredients critical to success for modern enterprise-*trust* and *know-how*.[19]

This definition is very important for two reasons. Firstly, it summarises the prevailing international approach of focusing on institutions able to respond to market and state failures instead of defending ourselves against the limitless deployment of the former—often seeking refuge in mutuals and cooperatives, but also predominantly in the state, as happened in the nineteenth and twentieth centuries.

Cooperatives are one updated form of response to political and market failures, with different characteristics, as I will outline later.

Secondly, we need to stress the link between the "service economy"[20] and the distinguishing features of mutual organisations. As opposed to the service economy, which concentrates intangible assets if fixed costs for the necessary long-term investments in human capital increase, mutuals operate through trust. They reduce transaction and control costs and[21] make every organisation financially efficient due to the value derived from personal skills. The thing that adds value is cognitive capital. This is consistent with its nature as an irregular and stochastic social and subjective phenomenon without economic ties that are too tightly determined, as is typical of the old economy (the new economy[22] has taken a decisive step towards a service society due to the emergence of the technological paradigm of Information Technology and Communication).

The resulting concept of enterprise and cooperative action is therefore much broader than a concept based on any form of economic organisation. It makes the community of destiny central to assumptions about human dignity, as defined by one of the most important proponents of the British cooperative Association, the wonderful Cooperative Council:

> the cooperative movement is founded on the belief that in your town, in your community, immediate solutions to the problems of work, debt, family instability and self-respect are in your hands; that the only solution in which you can really believe is one that you have outlined and for which you take responsibility. This is the cooperative spirit: women and men taking charge of the situation, responsible to one another, working through democratic control structures.[23]

A society of duties, therefore, rather than a society of rights.

These are undoubtedly the very democratic control structures identified as "mutual weaknesses",[24] based on an outmoded stance that is as old as the mutualist and cooperative movement itself.

The other more substantial weakness, if you will forgive the oxymoron, lies in the fact that it is more difficult for people-based companies to obtain finance than capital-based companies, but I will return to this later.

This revisitation of the cooperative ideal is global in scope. It began as a support network, growing from the roots of the original cooperative movement, combining tradition and modernity in a radical new cooperative alternative set against a framework of mutuality and intended as a response to the imperfections of market and state (and therefore the power, institutional and otherwise, of political classes, which are oligarchic in the sense intended by Michels[25]).

The most interesting research in this regard comes from the field of anthropology. I attempted to make my own contribution in a work published some years ago.[26] If we reflect on this intellectual output as it is handed down to us from original sources, we cannot help being struck by the simultaneous vein of tradition and modernity within the cooperative phenomenon unfolding before our eyes in the global arena. It is enterprise and social movement at the same time. The most thorough research, apart from some exceptions concerning Africa, are studies on the Indian cooperative phenomenon, which has its roots in British domination and arose during the nineteenth century, long before the 1957 ICA conference held in Kuala Lumpur that gave such a formidable boost to the Asian and African cooperative movement.[27]

Malcom Harper and Adrian Roy[28] stress in their research that cooperatives can only be successful if they respect certain constraints (which I will go into later) and if they avoid calling on the help of international philanthropic organisations—which is only useful during the initial start-up stage—and avoid having a state presence in management of the cooperative, that is as a permanently coercive form of control over the specific day-to-day activity of its organisational machinery. This does not imply that cooperative management must not be top-down. Rather, control must not be exercised in accordance with ineffective systemic organisational approaches but epidemiologically, in the same way as cultures and practices. Appropriate institutional and socialising instruments must be used together with local cultures, based on what is now long-established experience. We do not need to reinvent the wheel every time,[29] in the words of a work by Tushaar Shah that is very famous among proponents of the south-east Asian cooperative movement. This compares a "blueprint" model of institutional development with a "greenhouse" model. Both can be used, says Shah, but with caution and observance of local cultures: This incidentally touches on a major problem: the potential and ability to organise social intervention in order to galvanise the energies of local societies to help themselves and not depend on welfare. This is the approach adopted by Albert Maister based on community experiences in southern Italy implemented and theorised about with a pioneering spirit by Adriano Olivetti in the 1950s and 1960s.

Having guidelines, as is typical of the "blueprint" model, is indispensable when we want to establish new associations, irrespective of whether they are cooperative. However, it is essential to choose the most appropriate relationship to be established with the surrounding environment and the available personal resources within these guidelines. More than 100 years of experience with non-European cooperatives from America to Asia has shown us that cooperatives can be created and survive by following endogenous and exogenous pathways. Showing great pragmatism, Shah states: "They (cooperatives) evolve 'naturally', without external assistance…. (But) many companies come into being because their members are forced to do so through a process of top-down coercion and deceit…. Only a minority of cooperatives are genuinely endogenous in their origins and it is still unclear whether they can be longer lasting than those forcefully created exogenously".[30]

The lesson we can learn from this empirical, hands-on experience is that cooperatives are very different from one another in terms of management style and the reasons for their longevity.

The former are based on public and private philanthropic assistance; the latter are founded on the day-to-day creative efforts of their members, with all the resulting consequences on the shape of the cooperative enterprise and its loyalty to the principles of the International cooperative movement.

Building a cooperative experience in a society based on caste and tribal social groups[31] is of course very different from doing so in European or North American societies. After perusing the very interesting literature on this subject,[32] I feel bound to share Harper and Roy's acute observation: "We must remember that we are faced with a two-way process. A hospitable (or favourable) social and cultural environment can make all the difference in determining the success of a cooperative (according to principles of international cooperation), yet the success of corporation can play a very important role in creating a favourable environment". And this very aptly shows the role that "endogenous" cooperation can play as an agent of development.

Encouragingly, some studies stress that some cooperative development agents owe their longevity to the "critical factor" of members being able to make their own decisions about the business model, what they have to do and how they should go about it.[33]

One essential contribution to the theoretical reasoning behind this book has come from comparing the growing cooperative movement in emerging countries, Africa and south-east Asia (for which a substantial amount of research is available) and in historical settlement countries.

There is a striking similarity—despite enormous social differences between the historically determined environment in which the cooperatives grow up—between governance factors. In other words, the organisation is unvaried even on continents and in social environments far removed from the original international cooperation setting: old continental Europe and the evergreen transatlantic countries (US and UK).

An organ is created if there is a functional need for it, and like any good functionalist in the style of Durkheim, I can only rejoice in this discovery. It persuades me that a limited range of social factors is at play in human societies for achieving this aim, irrespective of the latitude or longitude in which those humans grow and group—this seems to be true irrespective of the enormous diversity of symbolic worlds and different connotations within which these factors are at play.

These social grouping factors are as follows: professional and ideological uniformity of the founders' backgrounds; similarity between professional skills; longevity of the leadership and its centralisation in a few hands (in traditional societies, the baton of leadership is very often passed from parents to children); significant flexibility of internal management rules to accommodate turbulence in the external environment; members' needs are met satisfactorily in accordance with shared rules of social support for them and their families.

Faced with this impressive consistency of factors, it is hardly surprising that Harper and Roy conclude their analysis (perhaps the most interesting I have come across while browsing studies on the cooperative movement), by stating: "Cooperatives are not always necessarily instruments of change; their members often come together to resist change and safeguard their interests … [the craftsmen of the Gouri tribe] are a classic example: management of the cooperative is passed on from father to son and members are able to continue with their age-old craft practices as they wish. The entry of new members is discouraged in most cases".[34]

We can take this impressive constancy as a starting point for our discussion of the non-capitalist affirmation of cooperation as both enterprise and social movement.

Overlooking the distinctive otherness of cooperative enterprise has been the most serious consequence of the utilitarian assumptions and bad advice that have driven neo-liberal restoration over the past 30 years.

Unlike capitalist enterprise, a cooperative is a partnership of people, not capital. A cooperative responds to shortcomings in the market and capitalist enterprise by pursuing the achievement of assets (work, consumption, credit and support) that could not be achieved individually.

A cooperative differs from public enterprise in expressing the collective ownership of more or less extensive groups and is not the outcome of a decision based on political sovereignty as are the diverse forms of public enterprise.

The purpose of cooperatives is not profit and appropriation of surplus but the pursuit of profit as a regulatory tool for management, designed to ensure continuity of the associated pursuit of work, consumption, credit and support assets.

The purpose of cooperation is to preserve and extend the social bond that breathed life into the enterprise. This social bond is a specific form of solidarity that oversees every cooperative action. The bond is not trade union-based because it aims to create an organisation with a stable effect on the market. The bond is not simply "benevolent" and not simply "non-profit" with regard to its economic and social regulatory structure: a cooperative is a specific form of enterprise that is socially managed with social goals, which have nothing to do with the activities of organisations that reformed neo-classicists or benevolent economists refer to as the "service sector" or social economy.

The factor of giving, that is of the gratuitous nature of the exchange, in a cooperative enterprise, lies in an extremely sensitive and valuable management mechanism: participation in decision-making through democratic systems for appointing managers (something that cannot happen in a capitalist enterprise) and meritocratic and technocratic control of management by the groups' collective owners, who are the members. These management mechanisms are shaped by interaction with and within the market. The cooperative does not remove itself from the market to act and fail undisturbed, when it would be relegated to a marginal role.

This is the reason why cooperation is both enterprise and social movement. Solidarity, idealism, mutual continuity are not secondary factors, but rooted in the specific form of its management. Cooperation as both enterprise and social movement is evidence that the economy is the outcome of personal histories and a set of relationships between people rather than reifying and alienating relationships between commodities. This set of interactions is not one-note but a symphony: different instruments help to shape the markets and the rules that determine them as well as their ongoing and irrepressible rejection of the stolid neoclassical, liberal model.

Cooperation is therefore a solidarity of hope, the reconstruction of an industrious community.

Other types of economic population organisations are active in imperfect markets in addition to capitalist enterprises and cooperative enterprises. These differ according to their allocation of the non-capitalist form of social ownership: for example, the non-profit sector often hides amidst a constellation of non-capitalist economic organisations that are of considerable importance in the social structure of each nation.

We speak indifferently of non-profit, third sector and voluntary organisations as though they were the same thing and, amidst this general confusion, these three terms end up identifying a marginal reality without any economic significance because it cannot have any assets or income.

Non-profit organisations are confused with voluntary organisations nowadays.

In actual fact, voluntary organisations are only one form of non-profit organisation, together with an entire series of "non-profit" companies that have an entrepreneurial structure and work mainly with assets and income in order to meet people's collective needs (education, health, school and culture).

The boundaries between non-profit organisations and voluntary organisations should not be blurred and neither can non-profit organisations be identified with the "third sector".

Non-profit organisations are therefore a third way between state and market. This expression is equivocal because it gives the idea of duality and substitution: space for non-profit organisations opens up in areas that cannot be reached by the state and where it is not economical for private enterprise to operate.

It is seen as a kind of inconvenient third party called upon to intervene and offer services only where other services cannot reach or have failed.

The problem lies in the fact that no positive concept of the non-profit phenomenon has ever been drawn up and it is often associated with the two definitions mentioned above, which prevents any understanding of its specificity and individual nature.

According to the System of National Accounts, non-profit organisations can be categorised as bodies "established for the purpose of producing goods or services, whose status does not allow them to be a source of income, profit or other financial gain for the units that constitute, control or finance them".

Non-profit bodies therefore deliver services that can be sold.

They can have assets and profits. The only constraint is that these should be reinvested in the structure.

Their scope may be mutualistic or public utility, aimed at people or the community. By their very nature, mutual structures are made up of families and businesses and provide services for their members.

Public utility, non-profit organisations provide services to people or the community: the latter category is made up of organisations, mainly derived from public institutions, which operate in sectors such as environmental, defence and security and compulsory social welfare services.

Public utility non-profit organisation providing services to people can be made up of public or private entities; their scope includes areas of social life such as health, education, welfare, culture and services at work.

Contrary to popular belief, this set of "moral economies", as I like to refer to it, is not a new phenomenon.

It is an age-old tradition all over the world, rooted in the great charitable institutions that arose during the Middle Ages and continues today through companies with cooperative titles that sit alongside non-profit organisations but differ from them radically even though they all stem from the great tradition of the moral economy.

The wealth of social works woven through civil history reflects people's creativity and their ability to join forces in order to come up with new responses to different needs.

This tradition is largely rooted in Roman Catholic apostolicism.

The Catholic Church has always put people, social formations and hence society before the state. It has identified the principle of subsidiarity as one of the cornerstones of its social doctrine. This principle establishes the role of intermediate communities, beginning with the family and ranging up to economic, social, political and cultural groups freely established by citizens, whose existence and action must be promoted and solicited by the authorities, not merely respected.

The first problem is to define moral economies.

These can be described as all activities stemming from people and things coming together with a view to a certain end. These must lead to the appropriation of profits by those who currently hold control and/or ownership of this association.

In the case of a cooperative enterprise, the profit is intergenerational and socially distributed through meritocratic participation.

An association of people and means with a view to a certain end is also commensurate with production of surplus, because if this does not come about, the association (which for now we will not refer to as an enterprise but a community in order not to confuse it with capitalist terminology) will not be able to reproduce itself. Unless the association is pervaded by obsessive statism, social self-reproduction can be determined merely by allocating part of the profit to the continuation of the association in accordance with civil and managerial rules.

In cooperation, for example, this profit is distributed in accordance with a group ownership approach and for intergenerational and collective purposes once self-reproduction has been achieved.

In voluntary organisations, once the purposes of self-reproduction have been achieved, nothing is left because no-one responsible for controlling and managing the association receives any salary or wages.

In this case, self-reproduction is accomplished by not allowing for any recompense for administrators and managers.

In non-profit associations, controllers and managers receive a one-off recompense, salary or wage according to self-allocated rules, and this recompense determines the need to ensure a form of governance—together with a purpose for the association.

Property rights are also allocated in moral economies. This can take very varied forms: a foundation whose assets are not private property; a form of allocation that is private or based on small groups who possess the means, methods and property and not for the distribution of surplus value or profit—and cooperatives.

The economic reality is therefore multifactorial: it is ruled by diversity.

It is organised on the basis of a symbolic system, spoken and unspoken beliefs and everyday ritual practices.

It is expressed through social organisations and the institutions that make these practices possible and ensure changes in and reproducibility of those practices.

It is expressed through personalities, cognitive frameworks and behaviours.

This is evident through studying companies in all their diversity as well as the consumption practices of human groupings.

It is essential to interpret relations with commodities and salaried work and cultural relations before the constituent objects are identified as objects.

All of us use things to build relationships that help us to give meaning to the transitional ages typical of an individual's life in ancient and modern societies.

This new conception of the global economy, of which the moral enterprise, that is the cooperative, is so much a part, begins with the revisiting of tradition: society becomes a community even in the world of commodities. And this makes us freer and less subjugated.

Faith?

For this dream to come true, we need to pursue an essential virtue of religious life: the evangelical scandal of utopia.

Utopia needs faith in human beings.

Faith is not a common commodity nowadays because its use is not non contestable, and it is very difficult to ensure it a form of governance typical of common goods.

The general assets of faith dry up when the inhabitants of the Earth turn their mental energies to the *polis*, or ideal city state, that is to the government by polyarchies. Polyarchies have always been a mixture of authority, power, terror and pragmatic acceptance. At some points in history, they have even involved consensus between rulers and the ruled and between elected representatives and electors in cases of non-dictatorial or semi-dictatorial democratic polyarchies. A polyarchy is a continuous interplay of absorbent and variable boundaries between democratic power and de facto situational power, which may be concerned with lobbying or corruption.

It governs the ever-shifting boundaries that economics and politics draw in the sand throughout the world as they intertwine in their rings of power.

Polyarchy changes according to the general gradations of faith in force.

The crisis in polyarchy as a general form of faith is being played out more or less convincingly throughout the world: in the old continent where historical parties are collapsing and ancient precedents of consensus and belonging are being eroded; in the new continent where the emergence of new cultures that were once marginalised, from black people to Latinos, is sparking deep divisions—and in South America, where the collapse of democratic consolidation is always a possibility due to the decline of ancient parties (APRA—*Alianza Popular Revolucionaria Americana – Partido Aprista Peruano*, American Popular Revolutionary Alliance – Peruvian Aprista Party—has disappeared in Peru, the face of Peronism has radically changed in Argentina, life in Colombia was always a matter of coexistence with ceaseless guerrilla warfare and has now achieved peace with the guerrillas that will have counterintuitive consequences). Even in South Africa, the party that gave freedom to black people is suffering from an unparalleled crisis of legitimacy.

The relationship between faith and legitimacy is a topic that has never appeared in scientific discussions of faith but is now exploding in our faces.

As soon as faith becomes an instrument of cohesion wielded by and within polyarchies, the link between this general or non-localised faith (believing in the rites of corner boys is a very different thing to believing in the Constitution) becomes very evident.

Faith is an obligation towards a person or people or body in whom the focus of personal or group expectations is invested, but also towards a more general body that or whom *we believe in*. The underlining is intentional. All parties subject to the relational mechanism of faith feel obliged to "believe". Having faith is never just trusting or not trusting; it is believing that moral limits exist in the behaviour of everyone making up the chain of faith that no-one can or wishes to breach.

Faith is always about belief.

For this reason, the greatest faith is faith in God and the greatest vocation is a religious vocation of dedication to this belief, which is strengthened when faith is commensurate with theodicy (the vindication of divine providence in view of the existence of evil), as the presence of Christ in the Eucharist is for Christians.

I believe that the faith ruling us today, that of monetary totalitarianism, has nothing to do with this faith and theodicy.

Theodicy is an apt term, because we can save ourselves in this world if we trust each other.

There is no salvation in faith in monetary transactions, but only profit, and the universal wells of faith, which are the true reservoirs of trust, will dry up if we believe this.

I believe that trust-based transactions performed without faith are leading us to exhaust the universal faith that the inhabitants of Earth have built up over thousands of years in order to allow human beings to live together.

This is already apparent in the loss of faith in polyarchic mechanisms and in the lost legitimacy of politicians representing social beings. Even the reproducibility of the family, a natural society, is increasingly challenged by the blurred boundaries of state monetary agencies. The family has fallen into a very deep crisis as demonstrated by the current demographic disasters, which are one of the causes of the world economic crisis.

There is not enough faith to go round to support the social division of work if the reproducibility of social and organic solidarity is halted, which is what is happening due to monetary totalitarianism. However, there *will* be enough for everyone if this totalitarianism can be stopped.

Our future challenge is to turn this faith into a potential common good in order to save society from self-destruction.

Notes

1. E. Mounier, *Révolution personnaliste et communautaire*, Paris, Éd. Montaigne, 1934, *De la propriété capitaliste à la propriété humaine*, Desclée de Brouwer, coll. "Questions disputées", 1936, *L'affrontement chrétien*, Neuchâtel, Éditions de la Baconnière, 1944, *Qu'est-ce que le personnalisme?*, Paris, Éditions du Seuil, 1947.

2. R. Guardini, *Opera Omnia. III/2, L'Uomo. Fondamenti di una antropologia cristiana* (edited by M. Borghesi? in partnership with C. Brentani), Morcelliana, Brescia, 2009.
3. M. Weber, *Economia e società. Vol. I*, Comunità, Milan, 1968, pp. 127–128.
4. H. Hansmann, *The Ownership of Enterprise*, The Balkan Press of Harvard University Press, Cambridge, MA, 1996.
5. Ibid., p. 3.
6. T. Geiger, *Demokratie ohne Dogma: Die Gesellschaft zwischen Pathos und Nüchternheit*, Szczesny, Munich, 1963.
7. G. Sapelli, *Coop, Il futuro dell' impresa cooperativa*, Einaudi, Turin, 2006.
8. .
9. I described the general history of the ICA in my book *La cooperazione. Impresa e movimento sociale*, Edizioni Lavoro, Rome, 1998, pp. 15–64.
10. .
11. V. Neale, *Proposal for an International Alliance of Friends of the Cooperative Production*, Macmillan, London, 1892.
12. C. Gide, *L' Alliance Cooperative Internazionale*, Editions Cooperative, Paris, 1905.
13. G. Sapelli, *La cooperazione, cit.*
14. H. Hansmann, *op. cit*, p. 21.
15. F.A. Angers, *La coopération: de la réalité à la theorie économique*, Fides, Montreal, 1974, p. 54.
16. Ibid., p. 58.
17. C. Leadbeater and Ian Christie, *To Our Mutual Advantage*, London, Denos, 1999.
18. C. Leadbeater and Ian Christie, *To Our Mutual Advantage*, London, Denos, 1999.
19. Ibid., pp. 7–8.
20. S. Illeris, *The Service Economy: A Geographical Approach*, Wiley, London, 1996; Vandermerwe, S. and Rada, J. (1988) "Servitization of business: Adding value by adding services", *European Management Journal*, vol. 6, no. 4, 1988.
21. See my: *Dolore e felicità*.
22. Inizio modulo.
    Fine modulo.
23. I. Hargreaves, *In From the Cold: Cooperatives and Social Exclusion* Cooperative Council, Manchester, 1999, p. 31.

24. C. Leadbeater and Ian Christie, *To Our Mutual Advantage*, *cit.*, pp. 21–23.
25. R. Michels, *Zur Soziologie des Parteiwesens in der modernen Demokratie. Untersuchungen über die oligarchischen Tendenzen des Gruppenlebens*, Werner Klinkhardt, Leipzig, 1911.
26. G. Sapelli, *Antropologia della globalizzazione*, Bruno Mondadori, Milan, 2002.
27. .
28. M. Harper and A.K. Roy, *Co-operatives Success. What Makes Group Enterprise Succeed*, Intermediate Technology Publication, London, 2000.
29. T. Shah, *Catalysing Co-operation*, Sage, New Delhi, 1996, pp. 232–233.
30. T. Shah, *Catalysing Co-peration*, *cit*, pp. 20–21.
31. One essential work of reference on this topic is: CENDERET, *Group Entrepreneurship and Rural Handcraft with the Rural Poor*, Center for Development and Research Training, Bhubaneswar, 1981.
32. H. Srivastava and M. Chaturvedi, *Rural Middlemen*, Ashish, New Delhi, 1986; R. Desai, *Farmer's Societies and Rural Development*, Chung, Allahabad, 1988.
33. M. Harper, *Their Own Idea. Lessons from Workers' Co-operatives*, It Publications, London, 1993.
34. M. Harper and A.K. Roy, *Co-operative Success. What Makes Group Enterprise Succeed*, *cit*, p. 140.

Bibliography

E. Mounier, *Révolution personnaliste et communautaire*, Paris, Éd. Montaigne, 1934, *De la propriété capitaliste à la propriété humaine*, Desclée de Brouwer, coll. "Questions disputées", 1936, *L'affrontement chrétien*, Neuchâtel, Éditions de la Baconnière, 1944, *Qu'est-ce que le personnalisme?*, Paris, Éditions du Seuil, 1947.

R. Guardini, *Opera Omnia. III/2, L'Uomo. Fondamenti di una antropologia cristiana* (edited by M. Borghesi in partnership with C. Brentani), Morcelliana, Brescia, 2009.

M. Weber, *Economia e società. Vol. I*, Comunità, Milan, 1968, pp. 127–128.

H. Hansmann, *The Ownership of Enterprise*, The Balkan Press of Harvard University Press, Cambridge, MA, 1996.

T. Geiger, *Demokratie ohne Dogma: Die Gesellschaft zwischen Pathos und Nüchternheit*, Szczesny, Munich, 1963.

G. Sapelli, *Coop, Il futuro dell' impresa cooperativa*, Einaudi, Turin, 2006.

G. Sapelli, *La cooperazione. Impresa e movimento sociale*, Edizioni Lavoro, Rome, 1998, pp. 15–64.

V. Neale, *Proposal for an International Alliance of Friends of the Cooperative Production*, Macmillan, London, 1892.

B. Gide, *L'Alliance Cooperative Internazionale*, Editions Cooperative, Paris, 1905.

F. A. Angers, *La coopération: de la réalité à la theorie économique*, Fides, Montreal, 1974, p. 54, 58.

C. Leadbeater and Ian Christie, *To Our Mutual Advantage*, London, Denos, 1999.

S. Illeris, *The Service Economy: A Geographical Approach*, Wiley, London, 1996; Vandermerwe, S. and Rada, J. (1988) "Servitization of business: Adding value by adding services", European Management Journal, vol. 6, no. 4, 1988.

G. Sapelli, *Il dolore e la felicità nelle organizzazioni*, in "Studi organizzativi", n. 1, 1999, pp. 87–102.

I. Hargreaves, *In From the Cold: Cooperatives and Social Exclusion* Cooperative Council, Manchester, 1999, p. 31.

R. Michels, *Zur Soziologie des Parteiwesens in der modernen Demokratie. Untersuchungen über die oligarchischen Tendenzen des Gruppenlebens*, Werner Klinkhardt, Leipzig, 1911.

G. Sapelli, *Antropologia della globalizzazione*, Bruno Mondadori, Milan, 2002.

M. Harper and A. K. Roy, *Co-operatives Success. What Makes Group Enterprise Succeed*, Intermediate Technology Publication, London, 2000.

T. Shah, *Catalysing Co-operation*, Sage, New Delhi, 1996, pp. 232–233.

CENDERET, *Group Entrepreneurship and Rural Handcraft with the Rural Poor*, Center for Development and Research Training, Bhubaneswar, 1981.

H. Srivastava and M. Chaturvedi, *Rural Middlemen*, Ashish, New Delhi, 1986.

R. Desai, *Farmer's Societies and Rural Development*, Chung, Allahabad, 1988.

M. Harper, T*heir own idea. Lessons from workers' co-operatives*, IT Publications, London, 1993.

4

Freedom and Diversity: The Anticapitalist Revolution

More on Allocation of Ownership

Nowadays the debate on the fate of the world economy increasingly includes a discussion of "natural rights to property": the unwritten law embodied in history through the life experiences of communities that were once described as "primitive". They have been gradually surrounded, more than incorporated, by the capitalist market and by societies such as the one in which we live.

In those societies, which also coexist in the general mode of capitalist production, communal forms of owning land or essential assets have come about for centuries without any written rights. Examples include fishing grounds and running water. They have been preserved for millennia due to this unwritten law.

These days, written law is typical only of societies born firstly of the law of trade and secondly of the law of parliament or judges.

Many of the topics covered here can be found in G. De Lucia Lumeno, G. Sapelli, *La rivoluzione è imminente: faremo comunque in tempo a prenderci un caffè*, Cantagalli, Siena, 2012.

G. Sapelli, *Beyond Capitalism*, https://doi.org/10.1007/978-3-030-20769-4_4

Andean communities, aboriginal communities, communities of the Slavic world, communities of the Brazilian landless, Chinese and Asian village communities and so on have now become exceptions to the expansion of the private law area. In large parts of the world, they stayed silent and allowed the reproducibility of de facto legal orders typical of this collective ownership.

This topic touches on the subject of common goods (or simply commons); in other words, goods that are defined as "public" not due to any form of state ownership, but because this form of ownership (not aimed at obtaining individual profit from the goods) is essentially cooperative, the property of small or large social groups and allow their reproducibility and use for all those who wish to gain access to them, in accordance with rules that ensure their infinite reproducibility.

Communities subject to unwritten ownership, as already mentioned, have allowed forms of human subsistence and environmental sustainability that would otherwise have been destroyed to be handed down for millennia.

Highly civilised societies have coexisted for centuries with such societies. Fortune has shone on the latter, providing a significant example for everyone, due to state or meta-state events involving the recognition of collective pre-capitalist rights and their legalisation as a kind of posthumous acknowledgement, as with the Australian aborigines, or conversion to collective ownership rights through written law rather than the customary de facto judicial orders.

This has happened in some cases in South America but, unlike the situation in Australia and New Zealand, here everything happened in a more politicised and conflicted manner, as in Brazil under the presidencies of Ferdinand Cardoso and Lula Da Silva.

The resulting broad field of reflection and study is unexpectedly topical for our capitalist economy, when we ask ourselves whether goods that have not yet been commodified should be considered common goods or whether they should be de-commodified, as is the case with water and protected areas of the environment (examples include beaches where sea turtles nest and breed, Amazonian resources and so on). There is an unexpected need to reflect on the different possible forms of ownership and the different ways of managing ownership even in the civil society we inhabit, submerged as it is in a deflationary and over-financialised economic crisis.

We need to ask ourselves the following question: how long will a market based on private assets allow the reproduction of goods essential for community life, such air purity, reformulation of employment standards and a type of landownership ensuring essential assets such as housing, for all the people of the earth?

What the financial market has destroyed, the community can rebuild.

In order to fully understand the extraordinary importance of common goods, they must form part of the debate that has taken place (I am sure it will now be resumed) over forms of allocating property rights. This matter came to a head in the animated and brutally honest debate that took place in 1997 at the Columbia School of Law.

The debate was ruthlessly heralded by the provocative title of the seminar to which the leading lights of North American corporate law had been invited: "Are Corporate Governing Systems Converging?"

The debate was bound to be dominated by Robert Charles Clark, due to the prestige of his research and his charisma, which strikes anyone who meets him.

His seminal works, *The Four Stages of Capitalism. Reflections on Investment Management Treatises* and *The Interdisciplinary Studies of Legal Evolution*,[1] both appeared at the very beginning of the fateful 1980s (the decade when neo-liberal financial globalisation took hold) and were a constant benchmark.

Now that the great global depression is questioning those very themes of corporate governance and principles of allocating ownership structures by organisational populations active in global markets and quasi markets, it is important to return to that extraordinary debate. Henry Hansmann and Reinier Krakmann referred to the event in paper that unfortunately passed unnoticed by most people when it was presented at a conference in honour of Clark that took place in 2005 at the Iowa University College of Law.

In my opinion, this essay is now crucial because of its scientific and political implications.[2]

Hansmann was the only world-renowned economist to reopen the debate on cooperative theory after a silence lasting approximately one century (after Pantaleoni, Rabbeno and Gobbi, who were all Italian … and Alfred Marshall), restoring scientific legitimacy to the existence and development of cooperative enterprises[3] and exploding the neoclassical fallacies rightly derided by Bruno Jossa.[4]

The essay referred to the theories of Francis Fukuyama,[5] who believed that the fall of the USSR led to history becoming a frictionless neo-liberalist and neo-liberal highway, with a form of capitalism that could be deployed without any social conflict or opposition like a set of gears that could turn freely due to the well-oiled market machinery.

The end of history as rending strife and unhappiness: the end of negative and dialectic philosophy, the triumph of celestial nothingness, the apotheosis of the capitalist enterprise and "shareholder value".

It is too easy to mock these theses. The reality is bad enough.

The thing that counts is the context. In the mid-1990s, it was taken for granted that we were about to overcome what the homeland of common law considered the three great forms of company governance and ownership, namely: "(1) a state-oriented model, (2) a labour (or, more broadly), stakeholder-oriented model (including the cooperative model as it is commonly understood), (3) a manager-oriented model)".[6]

We would allegedly see the overturning of each of these models (towards transformative convergence), which would be transcended by what Hansmann defined as: "The 'standard shareholder-oriented model' of the business corporation … on the most attractive social ideal (my underlining) for the organization of the large-scale enterprise".[7]

In some of his essays, Hansmann (the leading theoretician on cooperation) had already expressed great reservations about cooperatives and non-profit organisations being able to withstand the impact of globalisation. He believed that globalisation entails the drastic disappearance of levels of monopoly in the idiosyncratic supply of goods and services. According to his theories, the proprietary choice of a system of members-consumers-cooperators is the most effective approach due to the lowering of control and coordination costs typical of a user cooperative as opposed to a classic capitalist organisation.[8]

Hansmann was also influenced by theories that formed the basis for the cultural hegemony—hence the convergence he believed was inevitable—of the individual shareholders' capitalism[9] model.

It was a genuine social ideal of a macro-societal model, not merely a micro-entrepreneurial model. This should be remembered and stressed.

The managerial model separates ownership from control and therefore allows governance and the limitation and emergence of conflicts of interest when overcoming the social inefficiencies of correlated parties. It was also responsible for creating the gigantic wealth of our society during the two preceding centuries.

Capitalism that sets out to base itself on the guiding star of shareholder value does the opposite and unifies ownership and control, preventing any real form of governance that is not rhetorical.

The guiding star and unification aspects are not joined at the hip: they could arise separately. The important thing is that they have arisen together over the last 20 years.

Unification comes about through the totalitarian establishment of ownership capitalism,[10] when—as has happened in recent years—managers become capitalists and conflict of interest thus becomes an irretrievable part of globalised modern capitalism.

For this reason, not merely for any moral reason, stock options are a quintessential sign of this totalitarianism because they underlie the change and become an anthropological model of existence.

In a model of managerial capitalism where managers are held responsible for developing a business and capitalists reap the potential benefits of ownership, with the possibility of sacking the controllers of the enterprise if this benefit disappears, this mixture of management and capitalist ownership was and is considered a vice.

Due to "agency theory" whereby managers, who are considered to be immediately opportunistic by nature, are assumed to be only guided by material interests (if I were a manager, I would be ashamed and indignant of being treated in this way, however well-paid I was), this vice becomes a virtue.

Except that this virtue does not consider that the resulting great asymmetries of information between managers turned capitalists and capitalists who have remained capitalists (given that control of the corporation is quintessentially idiosyncratic) will ultimately relegate the capitalists and shareholders to being victims of the asymmetry of information and therefore succubae of the managers turned capitalists. Managers always know more than the shareholders about corporate governance and spend all their time making agreements with the leading lights of financial oligopolies (particularly investment banks and rating companies, with people from the same banks and great financial institutions sitting on their boards, thus institutionalising collusion and corruption) to increase the value of shares to their benefit instead of to the benefit of shareholders, as the events of the crisis ultimately demonstrated.

We need not waste any words on arguing my thesis. We need only think of what has been happening before our eyes. With the great global depression still going on, while shareholders have been reduced to playing out their allotted roles in this slaughter of the innocents, capitalist managers are still firmly at the helm of the companies whose dividends have been reduced to crumbs, except for occasional cases where some have broken the law and have been found out.

And no-one feels ashamed.[11]

Common Goods

Any convergence between the models would be truly devastating. Yet, and this is the point, convergence has not been total. Some protected species have escaped the big game hunters supporting the totalitarian appropriation of the theory and practice of shareholder value. The companies that have remained proudly standing are the ones that evade the bronze (i.e. by no means iron-clad) law of shareholder capitalism, primarily in their governance and manner of allocating ownership rights. In other words, situations where company managers are chosen based on family relationship tempered by meritocratic judgement, as in family firms, or appointed by shareholders meetings in a context of small-group ownership—as Max Weber described cooperatives.[12] Shareholders appoint managers, avoiding any form of bondage and limiting information asymmetries through discussion at shareholders meetings and personal relationships. In this respect, it is worth quoting a wonderful passage from a little-known speech by Hansmann delivered at the National Congress of Finish Cooperation in 1998, which remains a shining example:

> It is natural to ask what is responsible for this strong difference in governance between cooperatives and business corporations. It is tempting to respond that cooperatives are so responsive to their members because they can be. In many cooperatives, transactions between a typical member and the cooperative represent a substantial fraction of the member's income. This means that it is quite worthwhile for the member to invest heavily in becoming informed about the cooperative's affairs, which in turn permits the member to participate thoughtfully in elections to the board and other matters of cooperative governance. This is not the case, and the other hand, with all but the largest shareholders in a substantial-size business corporation.[13]

Family companies and cooperative enterprises therefore resist destruction, to the dismay of those who saw convergence as a social advantage and the coming of the "bronze law" as the end of a job well done.

The state does not behave as an owner and decision-making entity destined to die when it becomes technocratic but is rediscovered as a stakeholder in a last-ditch attempt to save what can be saved (a lender of last resort or nationaliser of last resort … but without any convergence).

Hansmann should have had more faith in himself and spoken out loud and clear to say that history has not ended, as he did in Finland to the members of the cooperative movement. Quite the contrary: it has just started.

The debate mentioned here and the recognition given to Ostrom are already a victory against the economic crisis, for freedom of thought and economic and civil action. A victory establishing a way out of the crisis founded primarily on "biodiversity" in economy: "biodiversity" beginning with enterprise because it is based on the multiplicity of being, the freedom of "social" and civil society before the state and hence the essence of what I call "polygamy of forms of exchange",[14] in other words the coexistence of different forms of company ownership, against any type of "one-track thinking" and "convergence". Only in this way can markets be less imperfect than they always actually are: that is, through competition generated by the multiple, simultaneous and contextual presence of different forms of enterprise.

This is because the heralded "convergence" has never been merely an intellectual plan or academic reflection throughout 20 years of totalitarian neo-liberal civil regression. Instead, it was a change at the top of the global economic system made in an attempt to reduce all the flora living in the global economy garden to an indistinct unity under the banner of shareholder value. It was a gigantic struggle for cultural hegemony.

This is why we must not confuse the order of events.

The economic crisis never caused the failure of this institutional and political (not economic) plan. It is a mistake to think that any organic mechanism is at work in the social fabric. Failure was the ideological outcome of allowing the reification of a market without values and without people. Luckily, this market only exists in the head of neo-classicists and the desire for power of the rulers of market hierarchies built institutionally through social exclusion, the inner circles of business schools and bad governance. This desire for power, which can call on very sophisticated intellectual resources and unlimited economic resources, all too often annihilates consciousnesses and minds in order to condition and shape institutions within and without the markets.

We can escape the moral and intellectual paralysis lying at the root of modern nihilism through communal subjectiveness and a revival humanism. One example of this is the resistance to convergence, standardisation and one-track thought demonstrated by the international cooperative world and primarily cooperative credit. This tendency transcends national boundaries. It is an extraordinary event, not a rearguard action or merely a national event.

Everything is encapsulated in the sad yet damning refutation of one of the paradigms of "convergent standardisation" by Garret Hardin, who some year ago coined the term "tragedy of the commons".[15] The tragedy whereby altruism is impossible, and fraternity is an illusion, giving rise to a climate of short-termism, stock options and a Pavlovian incentive model, is part of a universal anthropological paradigm.[16] If there is an asset that does not belong to private individuals or the state (e.g. an asset used for civic uses or the environmental assets that are theorised about a lot nowadays), there is inevitably a race to appropriate it in an individualistic manner and overexploit it to give rise to growing external diseconomies, benefiting from ownership but supporting only a small part of the cost (which is inevitably shouldered by society), thus devastating the assets: hence the inevitable tragedy.

Anthropology has confirmed and refuted this thesis innumerable times.[17]

In her seminal work,[18] Elinor Olstrom went one step further and demonstrated the existence of innumerable social constructs that can be used to prevent common properties degenerating and also make them sustainable in the long term. She also explained how we can improve their common management and effectiveness until they become genuine public assets, giving rise to institutions designed to guarantee their sustainability through cooperative behaviour and ultimately offering a third way between state and market: an approach involving democratic participation in management cleverly incentivised by drawing up shared rules that are continuously improved on and protected against free riders and the most subtle forms of opportunism.[19]

Merk Van Vugt aptly summarised the matter in a forthcoming paper due to be published by Kent University:

> The tragedy on commons has generated much research activity in the behavioural sciences, from psychology to political sciences and from economics to biology. But despite its compelling logic, it has been criticised for two main reasons. First, scientists studying real-word environmental problems have found many instances of successful community resource management projects around the world, such as maintenance of common agricultural land, irrigation systems, and lake and shore fisheries. Rather than a 'free for all', these commons are strictly regulated in term of access and intensity of use. A second more fundamental criticism concerns the validity of the assumption that commons users are driven exclusively by narrow (economic)self- interest. Although this is clearly an important motive, recent theoretical and empirical developments in social psychology, evolutionary biology, anthropology, and experimental economics suggest that individuals are not indifferent to the welfare of others, their group,

> or the natural environment ... researchers have discovered myriad motives beyond self-interest that influence decision making in commons dilemmas.[20]

Common goods (the commons) are one of the pillars of associated human life in extensive areas of the planet. Without them, neither market nor society can exist and only their proliferation can prevent social collapse, of which economic crises are simply one radical manifestation.

There is no public commodity more valuable than trust. There is no more satisfying form of serenity than simply being part of a community. This serenity overcomes nihilistic anomie, affirms its ideas by challenging politics, thus helping politics to become a civil virtue founded on debate and creating public spaces for people to meet and defend multiple forms of being and guarantee social development in freedom.

The virtuous principle of subsidiarity is an essential civilising factor today.

The question of a welfare society must be reconsidered in this light.

Notes

1. R. C. Clark, *The Four Stage of Capitalism. Reflections on Investment Management Treatises*, in "Harvard Law Review", n. 94, 561, 1981 and *The Interdisciplinary Studies of Legal Evolution*, "Yale Law Journal", issues 90, 1981.
2. H. Hansmann and R. Kraakman, *The End of History of Corporate Law*, in "Georgetown Law Journal", issue 89, 2001 and then reproduced in in J. Gordon and M. Roe (eds), "Convergence and Persistence in Corporate Governance", Cambridge University Press, New York, 2004.
3. Particularly thanks to H. Hansmann, *The Ownership of the Enterprise*, Harvard University Press, Cambridge, MA, 1996.
4. B. Jossa, *La teoria economica delle cooperative di produzione e la possibile fine del capitalismo*, Giappichelli, Turin, 2005.
5. F. Fukuyama, *The End of History and the Last Man*, Free Press, New York, 1992.
6. H. Hansmann, *How Close is the End of History?* in "Journal of Corporation Law", issue 31, 2006, p. 746.
7. Ibid.

8. I refer firstly to H. Hansmann, *Response to Review Essay of "The Ownership of Enterprise". Non-profit Organization in Perspective*, "Non-profit and Voluntary Sector Quarterly", issue 1, March 2000.
9. The most exemplary model of this theoretical excrescence, which was destined to pass into common belief with consequences similar to that of weapons of mass destruction (cognitive and behavioural), can be seen in M. Jensen and W. Meckling, *Theory of the Firm: Managerial* Behavior, Agency Cost and Ownership Structure, in "Journal of Financial Economics", issue 3, 1976.
10. R. Garruccio, *Managerialismo e antimanagerialismo. Trasformazioni culturali tra novecento e anni duemila*, in "Itinerari d' impresa", issue 11, 2007.
11. G. Sapelli, *La crisi economica mondiale. Dieci considerazioni, Postfazione di G. De Lucia Lumeno*, Boringhieri, Turin, 2009.
12. M. Weber, *Economia e società, vol. I*, Edizioni di Comunità, Milan, pp. 127–128.
13. H. Hansmann: *Cooperative Firms in Theory and Practice*, in "Finnish Journal of Business Economy", n. 1, 1999, p. 397.
14. G. Sapelli, *Introduzione*, to A. Salsano, "Il dono nel mondo dell' utile", Bollati Boringhieri, Torino, 2008, pp. 6–17 e G. Sapelli, *A dadiva na grande impresa capitalistica: trasformacao e reactualizacao*, in J.V. Serrao, M.de Avelar Pinheiro, M.de Fatima Sa e M. Ferreira, "Desenvolvimento Economico e Mudanca Social. Portugal nos ultimos dois séculos. Homenagem a Miriam Halperin Pereira", Imprensa de Ciencias Sociais, Lisboa, 2009, pp. 207–226.
15. G. Hardin, *The Tragedy of the Commons*, in *Science*, December 13, 1968.
16. A fine far-sighted profile of the hypostatisation of "convergent" philosophy in M. Hollis, *Models of Man. Philosophical Thoughts on Social Actions*, Cambridge University Press, Cambridge, 1977.
17. G. Sapelli, *Alternatives to marginalization: new forms of social action in Mediterranean towns*, in "Journal of Southern Europe and Balkans", vol. 2, n. 2, November 2000.
18. E. Ostrom, *Governing the Commons. The Evolution of Institutions for Collective Action*, Cambridge University Press, Cambridge, 1990.
19. For some essential reading, see E. Ostrom and J. Walker (eds), *Trust and Reciprocità: Interdisciplinary Lessons from Experimental Research*, Russel Sage Foundation, New York, 2003. M. Weber, S. Kopelman, D. M. Messing, *A Conceptual Review of Social Dilemmas: Applying a Logic of*

Appropriateness, in "Personality and Social Psychology Review", n. 8, 2004.

20. M. Van Vugt, *Averting the Tragedy of the Commons*, "Forthcoming Paper University of Kent", p. 5.

Bibliography

Many of the topics covered here can be found in G. De Lucia Lumeno, G. Sapelli, *La rivoluzione è imminente: faremo comunque in tempo a prenderci un caffè*, Cantagalli, Siena, 2012.

R. C. Clark, *The Four Stage of Capitalism. Reflections on Investment Management Treatises*, in "Harvard Law Review", n. 94, 561, 1981 and *The Interdisciplinary Studies of Legal Evolution*, "Yale Law Journal", issues 90, 1981.

H. Hansmann and R. Kraakman, *The End of History of Corporate Law*, in "Georgetown Law Journal", issue 89, 2001 and then reproduced in in J. Gordon and M. Roe (eds), "Convergence and Persistence in Corporate Governance", Cambridge University Press, New York, 2004.

Particularly thanks to H. Hansmann, *The Ownership of the Enterprise*, Harvard University Press, Cambridge, MA, 1996.

B. Jossa, *La teoria economica delle cooperative di produzione e la possibile fine del capitalismo*, Giappichelli, Turin, 2005.

F. Fukuyama, *The End of History and the Last Man*, Free Press, New York, 1992.

H. Hansmann, *How Close is the End of History?* in "Journal of Corporation Law", issue 31, 2006, p. 746.

H. Hansmann, *Response to Review Essay of "The Ownership of Enterprise". Non-profit Organization in Perspective*, "Non-profit and Voluntary Sector Quarterly", issue 1, March 2000.

M. Jensen and W. Meckling, *Theory of the Firm: Managerial* Behavior, Agency Cost and Ownership Structure, in "Journal of Financial Economics", issue 3, 1976.

R. Garruccio, *Managerialismo e antimanagerialismo. Trasformazioni culturali tra novecento e anni duemila*, in "Itinerari d' impresa", issue 11, 2007.

G. Sapelli, *La crisi economica mondiale. Dieci considerazioni, Postfazione di G. De Lucia Lumeno*, Boringhieri, Turin, 2009.

M. Weber, *Economia e società, vol. I*, Edizioni di Comunità, Milan, pp. 127–128.

H. Hansmann, *Cooperative Firms in Theory and Practice*, in "Finnish Journal of Business Economy", n. 1, 1999, p. 397.

G. Sapelli, *Introduzione*, to A. Salsano, "Il dono nel mondo dell' utile", Bollati Boringhieri, Torino, 2008, pp. 6–17.

G. Sapelli, *A dadiva na grande impresa capitalistica: trasformacao e reactualizacao*, in J. V. Serrao, M. de Avelar Pinheiro, M. de Fatima Sa e M. Ferreira, "Desenvolvimento Economico e Mudanca Social. Portugal nos ultimos dois séculos. Homenagem a Miriam Halperin Pereira", Imprensa de Ciencias Sociais, Lisboa, 2009, pp. 207–226.

G. Hardin, *The Tragedy of the Commons*, in "Science", December 13, 1968.

M. Hollis, *Models of Man. Philosophical Thoughts on Social Actions*, Cambridge University Press, Cambridge, 1977.

G. Sapelli, *Alternatives to marginalization: new forms of social action in Mediterranean towns*, in "Journal of Southern Europe and Balkans", vol. 2, n. 2, November 2000.

E. Ostrom, *Governing the Commons. The Evolution of Institutions for Collective Action*, Cambridge University Press, Cambridge, 1990.

E. Ostrom and J. Walker (eds), *Trust and Reciprocità: Interdisciplinary Lessons from Experimental Research*, Russel Sage Foundation, New York, 2003.

M. Weber, S. Kopelman, D. M. Messing, *A Conceptual Review of Social Dilemmas: Applying a Logic of Appropriateness*, in "Personality and Social Psychology Review", n. 8, 2004.

M. Van Vugt, *Averting the Tragedy of the Commons*, "Forthcoming Paper University of Kent", p. 5.

5

Against Rhetoric, Back to Theory and Struggle

Living Worlds ... Communities?

If this is the theoretical context we must inhabit to change the current capitalist society from technologies to values, what is going on in society, in the living world?

People are now crawling out of their abysses and back into action.

Some concepts need careful handling. Absolutely nothing is simple.

These concepts arise in a historically determined cultural climate and then, due to the lack of synchrony between culture and structure that always arises in any social construct, they slip out of the hands of those who seek to preserve their original value and take on another form and another meaning. They are like the Faustian genie that escapes from the bottle and flies up to lose itself in the sky of semantics to acquire a completely different yet equally important meaning. This is what happened with the concept of "community", starting with a seminal essay by Tonnies[1] at the end of the nineteenth century. This stated that community was the immediate relationship between individuals, whereas society was the division between roles that those individuals annihilated.

G. Sapelli, *Beyond Capitalism*, https://doi.org/10.1007/978-3-030-20769-4_5

Yet community could be resurrected through association and the fundamental paradigm of association in economy and markets: cooperation, a form of enterprise where the principle of community determined the rules of management and distribution of the wealth produced.[2]

Very little of that original line of thought has remained intact, even though it was very much ahead of its time and perceptive because like many works from different intellectual disciplines—we need only think of the reflection on de facto judicial systems by Santi Romano[3] (symbolic bonds of loyalty between groups, clans, forms of kinship[4] and so on) in the Italian Mediterranean, for example—it was written to explain the nature and irreversibility of the principle of association in modernity. Many believed that this modernity should be entirely determined by individual monism (the doctrine that only one supreme being exists) and a society based on roles: which would have destroyed the idea of community growing up in the wake of works by people like Summer Maine[5] ("from status to contract"), who believed that communities are merely a reflection of a segmented society. In his belief, the contract ended up becoming a transitive form to the simultaneous exclusion of all others.

Tonnies' theoretical premise, which is completely different from that of Summer Maine, postulated, in a spirit of Spencerian evolutionism, a fate marked by an uninterrupted path towards a kind of anthropological rather than legal obligation (a distinction we still fail to appreciate because this powerful thinker has been so poorly interpreted), founded on trade and its value in any action, that is his premise was that all actions are essentially economic.

Hence the compelling nature of the will to change: symbolic constructs became mandatory transactions between individuals, instead of relationships between people.

The community has never historically opposed the contract—just as the market has never opposed society, both historically caught up in a zero-sum game, as incorrectly envisaged by Polanyi,[6] when he described the birth of the welfare state as a kind of inevitable defence of society against the market. Polanyi believed that all societies under old and generally pre-capitalistic systems (see his studies on Central African society) had a socioeconomic formation that was overarchingly determined by ethics (noble and Judeo-Christian), which annihilated the market. Later, however, with the advent of the Industrial Revolution in Britain, the land enclosures and the growth of the proletariat and capitalist bourgeoisie, the social structure was entirely determined by the fully deployed market, with no place for morals and ethics in society, and market modulation became the exclusive task of the state.

Polanyi's theory is disproved by history: status is recreated in society, as it is society's role to recreate community and somehow slip in morals and ethics between the huge creases and slashes left in the social fabric by the cross stitches of the contract.

Status and community are continually being refreshed and revived. Only the blurred Ptolemaic glasses of neoclassical ideology prevent us from seeing this evergreen situation clearly through the Galilean telescope of the moral economy.

As we know, only Galileo's followers knew how to use his telescope.

As ever, the great founding father Durkheim[7] grasped everything: the social division of labour allowed this co-evolutionary coexistence between contract and status—community in society.

This is the conceptual crux of the matter: the mechanics of society and therefore the capitalist economy, which essentially shapes society's socio-economic structure, do not rule out the emergence of communities nowadays.

Quite the contrary: capitalistic society structures can act as the basis or existential condition of a community. In this case, non-profit associations and cooperatives that may be adopted as part of the systemic interrelationship, in accordance with criteria typical of well-modulated capitalist action, can offer such societal structures an essential lifeline through credit action or support for educational and technological innovation.

We can therefore define community in a manner relevant to our purposes: a form of ethical action, that is a sharing of goals by a group of people whose ethical spheres overlap for certain ends—allowing the development of social relationships that are not overarchingly determined by economic transactions but by the phenomenon of affective relationships, in the rational sense of the term (personal relationships).

This is possible because people are the only driving force that can unite community and society. Forging relationships with others for a given goal means that people need society and coexist in and with differentiation instead of with segmentation.

The latter form of liberal, neoclassical hypostatisation recognises only individual Robinson Crusoes, preventing any understanding of the coexistence of otherness.

People: Our Strength

People are the only force able to combine roles, hence society and personal relationships, hence community. Buber[8] understood this mystically and cabalistically based on an esoteric Jewish approach, which Adriano Olivetti[9] (to whom I will return) implemented as a modern, redeeming saint, through enterprise and a social life civilised by labour liberated from the alienation and ideology of exploitation.

Tonnies was describing this situation ahead of his time when he wrote of his amazement at seeing workers found cooperatives rather than allow themselves to be tangled in Bismarckian welfare models and poor people standing in the front line against marginalism and self-government.

In his marvellous, seminal book, society failed to destroy community, actually drawing strength from it. Hirsch[10] also taught us that a market without moral support not only fails to develop but also actually ceases to exist.

Interpersonal and group relationships therefore constitute a strong, deep warp thread, in all the shifting colours of lives lived in association.

Simmel[11] saw this come about with the circulation of money, understanding that a force that he initially believed was only destructive actually brought people together and released energy instead of annihilating it. Money united instead of divided due to the degrees of freedom for social constructions it was able to trigger.

The quintessence of the symbolic contract—currency—frees people from the inadequacy of barter and multiplies its symbolic intrinsic force without losing any of the beauty of the personal relationship, as demonstrated by the experience of cooperative banking, for example, and the trust that allows this to become established and spread.

The fundamental concept emerging from all this is that of a community that could coexist with society and not necessarily have to be nurtured by it; segmentation is recreated out of differentiation: this is the arcane secret.

This leads us back to the very powerful concept of the gift: the all-embracing and significant power of giving that is inherent in beings.[12]

The great writer Le Play,[13] in his seminal essays on the family—written with Chajanov,[14] a Menshevik economist, sociologist and anthropologist—taught that we should not come to an intellectual full stop at the concept of family as a natural society. Instead, we should seek to understand its development by stripping away the biological aspects in order to examine its economic aspects and the way it develops as part of an essentially sociological differentiation to revive the idea of a highly segmented structure, as is typical—today as in the past—of the idea espoused by contemporary economists and politicians that the family acts as an economic unit.

The *oikos* (the family, the family's property and the house) thus becomes a new approach to the idea of community that we talk about these days without any understanding, a perfect example of the perennial Hegelian spirit of the relevance of thought without any conceptual basis.

The family as an economic unit (embraced conceptually as the paradigm of an economic action with a moral basis) is an exclusively intellectual construct. Like the Santa Barbara fault line, this neoclassical, transactional and utilitarian ideology could give way at any moment, but its guardians are oblivious (perhaps just as well for them).

Social relationship is therefore the secret.

Relationship is not merely face to face: it is primarily symbolic and concerned with remembrance, part of the narrative of thought.

The great Romanist philologist Leo Spitzer[15] taught us about the greatness of the symbolic construct of the family community, neighbourhood and nationality by collecting—in a labour of love—letters written by Italian soldiers during World War I to families and loved ones who waited, hoped, prayed and suffered.

Leo Spitzer followed an exemplary trajectory: beginning with World War I, he began to draw up a new symbolic concept of community based on collective memory in the style of Halbaswch.[16]

He had tapped into a wellspring that took him back to the source of an underground river in the form of his collection of preserved oral memories. The community revealed by the exchange of letters is also commemorated in the letters of Polish peasants: *The Polish peasant in Europe and America* by Thomas and Zanieski[17] makes fascinating and prescient reading. They anticipated what would happen in the terrible years of dictatorship when the flower of world intelligence embodied in Jewish thought fled from Nazi Germany. The conception of community was to cross the Atlantic, from Europe to North America, and there begins a new life. From that time, it can be conceived as a symbolic cloud transcending physical form to become a construct of the soul.

A Jungian archetype in the face of Freudian biological primitivism.

Leo Spitzer used his letters and correspondence-based history (learned from Mattenklott,[18] whose mastery is undimmed by death), as a starting point to show that language becomes an emblem of spiritual community for anyone who wishes to speak it and interpret it. It was a remotely conducted way of keeping the community over the ocean alive, through memory and the language of letters: family and neighbourhood assets, matrimonial strategies and youthful destinies, participation in non-family and national choices and so on.

The great names of North American sociology, Parson[19] and Riesman[20] (who came after the Chicago school of sociology, which reduced the concept of community to the dry theory of demographic and quantitative research, though we have fortunately emerged unscathed from this period of paralysis), gave us a fascinating portrait of this community, torn apart by the anguish of modernity.

Riesman told us of the sense of loneliness among the crowd and therefore of the loss of community that throws the soul into anomie. Parson wrote about the concept of latency and symbolic structural cohesion underpinning the cultural self-attribution that allows individuals to find their place in the social strata, thus showing us a new Durkheimian approach destined to outlive every contemporary conflict and schism.

In latency, as in the escape from anomie, age-old links are ultimately reforged and strengthened by establishing relationships that transcend all kinds of boundaries: a community that lives at a distance and can become nostalgia and a community of destiny, thus regaining its true and profound existential meaning.

Notes

1. F. Tonnies, *Gemeinschaft und Gesellschaft*, Leipzig: Fues's Verlag, 2nd ed. 1912.
2. I have studied this topic throughout my career. See G. Sapelli: *La cooperazione come impresa: mercati economici e mercato politico*, in (a cura di G. Sapelli), "Il movimento cooperativo in Italia. Storia e problemi", Turin, Einaudi, 1981, pp. 254–349. *La C.M.B. e la sua storia (1904–1976). Integrazione, organizzazione e sviluppo: la specificità cooperativa*, in "Impronte. Testimonianze del lavoro della Cooperativa Muratori e Braccianti di Carpi dal 1920 ad oggi", Modena-Megaron, 1983, s.i.p.

   La cooperazione dalla crisi economica alla teoria dell'impresa (Una nota antineoclassica), in "Economia e politica industriale", issue 42, 1984, pp. 30–57. *Costruire l'impresa. La CMC di Ravenna dal 1945 al 1972*, Bologna, 1991, p. 239. *La cooperazione: impresa e movimento sociale*, Edizioni Lavoro, Rome, 1998, p. 182, subsequently be published with the cup forward by G. De Lucia Lumeno, da Go Ware Firenze, 2015 *Cooperazione, proprietà, management. Il modello CCPL*, Libri Scheiwiller, Milan, 2004. *COOP. Il futuro dell' impresa cooperativa*, Einaudi, Turin, 2006.
3. F. Santi Romano, *L'ordinamento giuridico*, Giunti, Florence, 1946.
4. M. Godelier, *Metamorphose de la parentè*, Fayard, Paris, 2004.
5. H. Sumner Maine, *Ancient Law – Its Connection With The Early History Of Society And Its Relation To Modern Ideas*, Cambridge, London, 1996.
6. K. *Polanyi*, foreword by R. M. MacIver, *The great transformation*, Beacon Press, Boston, 1957.
7. E. Durkheim, *La divisione del lavoro sociale*, Edizioni di Comunità, Torino, 1982.
8. M. Buber, *Il principio dialogico*, tr. P. Facchi and U. Schnabel, Comunità, Milan, 1959.
9. G. Sapelli, *La santità di Adriano Olivetti*, in, G. Sapelli, D. Cadeddu, "Adriano Olivetti. Lo spirito nell' impresa", Il margine, Trento, 2007, pp. 37–50.
10. F. Hirsch, *I limiti sociali allo sviluppo*, Bompiani, Milan, 1980.
11. G. Simmel, *Philosophie des Geldes*, Leipzig: Duncker & Humblot, 1900.
12. G. Sapelli, (under the pseudonym of Mauricio Plessiée), *Il dono nella grande impresa capitalistica e le forme dello scambio*, in "Studi organizzativi", n. 3, 1999, pp. 47–60 and again G. Sapelli, *Introduzione*, to

A. Salsano, "Il dono nel mondo dell' utile", Bollati Boringhieri, Torino, 2008, pp. 6–17 e G. Sapelli, *A dadiva na grande impresa capitalistica: trasformacao e reactualizacao*, in J.V. Serrao, M. de Avelar Pinheiro, M. de Fatima Sa e M. Ferreira, "Desenvolvimento Economico e Midanca Social. Portugal nos ultimos dois séculos. Homenagem a Miriam Halperin Pereira", Imprensa de Ciencias Sociais, Lisboa, 2009, pp. 207–226.

13. F. Le Play, *L'Organisation de la famille: selon le vrai modèle signalé par l'histoire de toute les races et de tous les temps*, Alfred Mame, Tours, 1907.
14. A. Chajanov, *Die Lehre von bäuerlichen Wirtschaft. Versuch einer Theorie der Familienwirtschaft im Landbau*, Paul Parey, Berlin, 1923.
15. A. Chajanov, *Die Lehre von bäuerlichen Wirtschaft. Versuch einer Theorie der Familienwirtschaft im Landbau*, Paul Parey, Berlin, 1923.
16. M. Halbwachs, *Les cadres sociaux de la mémoire*, Paris, Presses Universitaires de France, 1952.
17. T. I. William, Z. Florian *Il contadino polacco in Europa e in America*, Edizioni di Comunità, 1968.
18. G. Mattenklot, *Über Juden in Deutschland*, Jüdischer Verlag, Frankfurt am Main, 1992.
19. T. Parsons, *The Structure of Social Action: A Study in Social Theory with Special Reference to a Group of Recent European Writers*, Free Press, New York, 1968.
20. D. Riesman, N. Glazer, R. Denney *The Lonely Crowd: A Study of the Changing American Character*, Todd Gitlin (Foreword by), Yale University Press, 1950.

Bibliography

F. Tonnies, *Gemeinschaft und Gesellschaft*, Leipzig: Fues's Verlag, 2nd ed., 1912.

G. Sapelli: *La cooperazione come impresa: mercati economici e mercato politico*, in (a cura di G. Sapelli), "Il movimento cooperativo in Italia. Storia e problemi", Turin, Einaudi, 1981, pp. 254–349. *La C.M.B. e la sua storia (1904–1976). Integrazione, organizzazione e sviluppo: la specificità cooperativa*, in "Impronte. Testimonianze del lavoro della Cooperativa Muratori e Braccianti di Carpi dal 1920 ad oggi", Modena-Megaron, 1983, s.i.p.

La cooperazione dalla crisi economica alla teoria dell'impresa (Una nota antineoclassica), in "Economia e politica industriale", issue 42, 1984, pp. 30–57.

Costruire l'impresa. La CMC di Ravenna dal 1945 al 1972, Bologna, 1991, p. 239. *La cooperazione: impresa e movimento sociale*, Edizioni Lavoro, Rome, 1998, p. 182, subsequently be published with the cup forward by G. De Lucia Lumeno, da Go Ware Firenze, 2015 *Cooperazione, proprietà, management. Il modello CCPL*, Libri Scheiwiller, Milan, 2004. *COOP. Il futuro dell' impresa cooperativa*, Einaudi, Turin, 2006.

F. Santi Romano, *L'ordinamento giuridico*, Giunti, Florence, 1946.

M. Godelier, *Metamorphose de la parentè*, Fayard, Paris, 2004.

H. Sumner Maine, *Ancient Law – Its Connection With The Early History Of Society And Its Relation To Modern Ideas*, Cambridge, London, 1996.

K. Polanyi, foreword by R. M. MacIver, *The great transformation*, Beacon Press, Boston, 1957.

E. Durkheim, *La divisione del lavoro sociale*, Edizioni di Comunità, Torino, 1982.

M. Buber, *Il principio dialogico*, tr. P. Facchi and U. Schnabel, Comunità, Milan, 1959.

G. Sapelli, *La santità di Adriano Olivetti*, in, G. Sapelli, D. Cadeddu, "Adriano Olivetti. Lo spirito nell' impresa", Il margine, Trento, 2007, pp. 37–50.

F. Hirsch, *I limiti sociali allo sviluppo*, Bompiani, Milan, 1980.

G. Simmel, *Philosophie des Geldes*, Leipzig: Duncker & Humblot, 1900.

G. Sapelli, (under the pseudonym of Mauricio Plessiée), *Il dono nella grande impresa capitalistica e le forme dello scambio*, in "Studi organizzativi", n. 3, 1999, pp. 47–60 and again G. Sapelli, *Introduzione*, to A. Salsano, "Il dono nel mondo dell' utile", Bollati Boringhieri, Torino, 2008, pp. 6–17 e G. Sapelli, *A dadiva na grande impresa capitalistica: trasformacao e reactualizacao*, in J. V. Serrao, M. de Avelar Pinheiro, M. de Fatima Sa e M. Ferreira, "Desenvolvimento Economico e Midanca Social. Portugal nos ultimos dois séculos. Homenagem a Miriam Halperin Pereira", Imprensa de Ciencias Sociais, Lisboa, 2009, pp. 207–226.

F. Le Play, *L'Organisation de la famille: selon le vrai modèle signalé par l'histoire de toute les races et de tous les temps*, Alfred Mame, Tours, 1907.

A. Chajanov, *Die Lehre von bäuerlichen Wirtschaft. Versuch einer Theorie der Familienwirtschaft im Landbau*, Paul Parey, Berlin, 1923.

M. Halbwachs, *Les cadres sociaux de la mémoire*, Paris, Presses Universitaires de France, 1952.

T. I. William, Z. Florian *Il contadino polacco in Europa e in America*, Edizioni di Comunità, 1968.

G. Mattenklot, *Über Juden in Deutschland*, Jüdischer Verlag, Frankfurt am Main, 1992.

T. Parsons, *The Structure of Social Action: A Study in Social Theory with Special Reference to a Group of Recent European Writers*, Free Press, New York, 1968.

D. Riesman, N. Glazer, R. Denney *The Lonely Crowd: A Study of the Changing American Character*, Todd Gitlin (Foreword by), Yale University Press, 1950.

6

Blowing into the Bottle

Adriano Olivetti and the Language of Hope

In a world that ignores historical memoirs, lacking a culture of community where men and women can relate to one another through association with all their personal quirks, words are very often used inappropriately and men such as Adriano Olivetti are mentioned without knowing anything about their true thoughts.

Thirty-four years ago, on 27 February, Adriano Olivetti concluded his great adventure as the first Italian entrepreneur when he died of cerebral thrombosis on a train from Milan to Lausanne. He was an industrialist from the Canavese area of Italy who bought out a US company, Underwood, and played a leading role in establishing the first substantial information technology supply chain. Olivetti was a great entrepreneur, but the secret of his experience was his interior life, his intellectual references, what was once referred to as his soul (a term belonging to the philosophy of Christian personalism no longer used today). Olivetti was also a great publisher. He set up a publishing company named 'Comunità', with the aid of some worthy contributors, who then went on to make

G. Sapelli, *Beyond Capitalism*, https://doi.org/10.1007/978-3-030-20769-4_6

great contributions to Italian culture: Alessandro Pizzorno, Geno Pampaloni, Paolo Volponi and many more.

We cannot understand his personal interpretation of the concept of community without reference to the term as Giuseppe Berta used it in his book, which nevertheless dealt only with Olivetti's practical achievements: town planning, the theoretical reformulation of human relations and his ideas of management as company reform and the achievement of human freedom within business. This side of Olivetti is essential, but he also harboured a hidden, esoteric side. This was the utopian Olivetti. He was a utopian in a specific sense. What is utopia? It is an idea that can be prefigured in the here and now while people live and do, exercising their duties and rights; a different world people can believe in and expect to be better than the one they now inhabit in association with others. To understand the utopian basis of Olivetti's thought, we need to understand his family background and particularly the role of his father Camillo Olivetti. Camillo is part of the history of Italian entrepreneurship, since he was the acknowledged father of the precision mechanics industry. He is also part of political history, because he organised Turati's escape to exile from fascist Italy. He lived his life tormented by a quintessentially religious problem. He was a Jew and by the end of his life, he had reached a kind of syncretic compromise between the two religions of the Bible, the Christian religion and the Jewish religion. He ultimately joined the Unitarian Church, which aimed to combine the spirit of Jewish culture with the spirit of Christian tradition.

By the mid-1920s, Olivetti had already visited the US and had written some extraordinary works. I studied these many years ago, setting out my views on his ideas of corporate organisation in a book published in 1978 by Rosenberg and Sellier. Olivetti was immersed in business practice, particularly in technological practice (he founded a magazine that is still very important today entitled "Tecnica ed organizzazione"), but he also lived in a family where religion was all-important and pondered the fate of the world from an eschatological viewpoint. Olivetti's idea of history was typical of his Jewish culture. A few years ago, Stéphane Mosès published a book entitled *The Angel of History* (inspired by the famous phrase of Walter Benjamin), describing a new vision of history formulated by three great Jewish thinkers: Franz Rosenzweig, Walter Benjamin and Gershom Scholem. What was the fundamental premise? The book counters an optimistic post-Hegelian view of history with the different ideas of these three thinkers, referring to three different strands of Jewish thought: Scholem referred to the Kabbalah, Benjamin to the German tradition perpetuated by the Frankfurt school and Rosenzweig to a classically religious school of thought. These three intellectuals essentially saw historical events and the notion of historical progress as something that could be interrupted at any given moment through ruptures created by human actions, which by the simple fact of taking place heralded messianic redemption: the coming of the Messiah.

I find myself reading more and more these days out of my general disgruntlement with reality and came across this passage in the first volume of the complete works of Simone Weil. It is part of a small article entitled "Ethics and religion": "A virtuous man must do his duty [here she quoted Pascal] and leave the gods alone. He must not desire success but want duty. Yet he must accept his success as the purpose of his free act. It is contradictory to want action without wanting this action to be effective. Anything that is truly a virtue cannot be achieved without the action being effective, precisely because the value of the action lies only in its effectiveness. Wanting action and not wanting its effect is wanting without courage, it is not wanting". This passage holds the key to understanding the meteoric Adriano Olivetti, who was one of the very few people to hold enormous economic and intellectual power and use it to try to change the direction of history in accordance with what were essentially his own views and ideas. Simone Weil was a writer who Olivetti introduced to Italy. She was a Jewish mystic (pupil of one of the great French philosophers, Alain) and died during World War II after working as a labourer and fighting in the Spanish Republican war. She succumbed to hardship and hunger in London, ever faithful to her principles of solidarity. Like Olivetti, she was a person of Jewish origin who felt an affinity with Catholicism.

In a religious sense, Olivetti belongs to the tradition of Jewish messianism because he saw action as the vindication of divine providence. For most people, however, nothing could be further from a spiritual life than industry. Industrial activity is essentially mechanistic. Olivetti's purpose was to fill the industry with spirituality. He was a man who tried to reconcile action with wanting its effects, but an eschatological sense consistent with his deeply spiritual messianic outlook. What did Olivetti set out to do? He continued to work in the field where he and his father reaped their first successes in the field of precision mechanics. In the last years of his life (which ended in an almost divine act, because it was so unexpected and tragic), he entered the extraordinary industry of information technology. He wished to radically reform the industrial fabric of Italy and the relationship that existed between industry and society. The person who best expressed Olivetti's messianic view of history was Felice Balbo, an intellectual who offered an indispensable understanding of Olivetti's mysterious, utopian and religious side.

Count Balbo di Vinadio was born in 1913 in Turin. He attended a famous high school, where he was taught by Augusto Monti. His classmates were Franco Antonicelli, Cesare Pavese and Massimo Mila. He was an officer in the 1940 Russian campaign, but became ill and returned from the front in 1941, when he began his intellectual work. He was part of a small group of friends within the publishing company Einaudi. They coalesced around Giaime Pintor, the group's rising star, who wrote an extraordinary book entitled *Il sangue d'Europa* and was killed in a mine explosion when he was about to join his first battle in the partisan ranks. Balbo was the founder of Catholic communism, a very important strand of the Christian left-wing that grew up in an attempt to unite Marxist humanism and Christian humanism. He wrote a very important book entitled *Il laboratorio dell'uomo* but was mainly known for publishing *Le idee per una filosofia dello sviluppo umano* when he was practically on his deathbed. His themes chime extraordinarily with the ideas Olivetti held dear, but they lived separate lives and met only rarely: their personalities were too strong for them to get along with one another. Balbo was nevertheless to play a very important role because he was responsible for establishing managerial studies at Italy's state Istituto per la Ricostruzione Industriale (IRI). At the beginning of the 1950s, he brought US managerial thinking to Italy, together with Glisenti.

What did Balbo write? He concluded his work *Le idee per una filosofia dello sviluppo umano* with this passage, which defines the practical context of fulfilment through action that Simone Weil referred to and Olivetti used as his guiding light. These words date from 1962 but could have been written today: "In Italy, the industrial situation is not the same as in America, which sees human relations and the systematic education of human groups as natural requirements for ensuring economic dynamism. One of the major problems with today's American economy is that of maintaining profit levels and ensuring corporate survival. However, in Italy we have more serious and ingrained problems. We must set out to rouse as many of these separate and isolated subordinate energies as possible to social action and make managers in charge aware of this problem. Until now, everyone has been, for the most part and in different ways, ignorant of the most vital aspects of industrial civilisation, while some of its worst consequences (the dehumanisation of industrial labour) are now being unremittingly felt. Instead of or in addition to the problems experienced by America, the Italian economy has the problem of reducing social liabilities or making social expenses productive. This is all the more keenly felt because these social expenses are not exceptional but tend to increase, spread and become established because the human masses must now turn their energies to becoming active and productive or settle for being maintained in the most disparate ways, even in extreme poverty". The choice is between productivity and a welfare dependency culture, said Balbo, but productivity can only be achieved by human fulfilment through industry: "The topic discussed here seems to be one of the most relevant to the study of these overdue tasks". Like Olivetti, his ideas of social development and economic development coincided with those of human development. He wrote, in his philosophical style: "Human development and therefore the fulfilment of humanity as humanity". And with reference to Feuerbach: "Social development is the fulfilment of society in accordance with the human essence". Olivetti's work began from this starting point: how to organise society according to the human essence, the essence of people and the defence of people's integrity and personal fulfilment. He began to reflect on "community".

Before briefly mentioning his extraordinary book *L'ordine politico delle Comunità*, an exceptionally forward-thinking work that someone should have the courage to republish, I would like to mention Emanuel Mounier, who taught Olivetti his ideas of community. Mounier was a thinker whose book entitled *Rivoluzione personalista e comunitaria* was published by Edizioni di Comunità, the publishing company owned and managed by Adriano Olivetti. Together with Maritain, Mounier was one of the great prophets and thinking spirits of twentieth-century Catholicism. Maritain lived long enough to become an adviser to Pope Paul VI during the Second Vatican Council before dying prematurely. He founded the journal of the French Catholic left-wing *Esprit*, which is still required reading for anyone who wishes to gain an all-round cultural education. This book contains notes and reflections expressing some fundamental concepts known to Olivetti. Mounier believed that for Christians the political world and the economic world must be subordinate to the moral world, the moral world must be subordinate to the metaphysical world and the metaphysical world must be subordinate to the supernatural world. There must be a strict hierarchy and worldly conventions are not what counts (see the connection between Jewish messianism mentioned earlier and Mounier's Christian messianism). The thing that counts is fulfilling the Gospel in history and the subordination of the economy to the moral sphere, respecting the distinction between spheres: this is a reworking of Thomism (the theology of Thomas Aquinas). There is subordination, and there is a hierarchy, but there is no interpenetration. The economy has its own rules, but it must be subordinate because it is an end and not a means. It must not be subordinated to the moral of means: the means is global autonomy.

What was the only viable viewpoint, according to Mounier? The socialist and Christian view (which he saw as communist, in the sense of being a communion of goods and property) were in balance. How should this hierarchy of politics and the economy be achieved with regard to the moral and supernatural spheres? This could be done transparently, in a political and economic body that Mounier stated to be "decentralised", down to the level of individual people. It could not be achieved through top-down statism but had to be built up (within a network of cultural references including Balbo): "We will attempt to break down power into a series of communities, some on overlapping levels, inter-regulated by the principal of arbitration, others dependent although each preserving a certain amount of autonomy. When a larger power [the State in this case] tends to abuse its authority, intermediate communities on the sidelines will call it to order. When the individualism of individuals or small communities tends to open up an anarchic gap, the same intermediate communities will recall them to their social duties". A Thomist principle is therefore at work in this case, that is the principle of subsidiarity, which states that an organ far moved from the function must not do what a nearby organ can do. The basic idea of the principle of subsidiarity is even discussed within the European Economic Community nowadays, which all goes to show that Olivetti's ideas of expressing oneself through action are as fresh as ever.

What is the underlying idea? We begin to see that economic and political power must be broken down and organised in a context with the person at the centre. The person is a fundamental concept: we are not speaking about the individual. There is a radical difference between the concept of the individual and that of the person. In the writings of Mounier and Olivetti, the latter refers to the individual as having the moral integrity typical of a moral person and capacity for fulfilment; the State in which he lives or the society with which he is most directly interrelated must offer him opportunities to fulfil himself. An individual is seen as an indivisible whole, who only believes in achieving immediate benefit and therefore lacks moral integrity. An individual is selfish, a Hobbesian being in a state of nature who, without the Leviathan of state, behaves like a wolf among wolves. A person is an individual with moral balance. This is an idea of Mounier's that pervades all Olivetti's thoughts: "Only a partially collective organisation such as the one we hope will be based on a collective of people [the basic communities], who assume various degrees of accountability can allow the salvation of these values [i.e. personal value], adapting them to the material conditions of our age". Olivetti then went on to express the same thought in a more complicated institutional language in *L'ordine politico della Comunità*.

In this work, Olivetti clearly stated that the community should own part of the enterprises, hence they should be self-managed by the community in accordance with socialist ideas. Olivetti's communities bore no relation to the communities we are theorising about today. His was an anti-liberalist, not an anti-liberal community (we should always remember Benedetto Croce's distinction between economic liberalism and political liberalism): liberal principles in politics are one thing but liberal principles in economics are another. Mounier talked about "management of capital" as the "reabsorption of capital into the hands of the workers and organisers in charge [i.e. managers]. The benefits were to be divided into four sectors once general corporate services had been guaranteed (uniform wage, sliding scale, profit-sharing, benefits from life annuities set aside for pensions and so on, credit organisation and control [which would have to be carried out on a community scale], legal suppression of all forms of usury, speculation and any form of interest-bearing investment in general)". Also: "In the management of production: collective control, not state-centred but decentralised with state participation in enterprises that are important enough to take on the nature of genuine public services. Organisation of all other companies into federal production communities. Orientation of the economy toward real needs and the greater dissemination of common goods rather than towards profit and the infinite growth of the comforts of well-being". I mention this because nowadays we talk a lot about the limits of development and self-regulated development. These are ideas that Christian personalist thought espoused back in the 1930s: respect for the environment, respect for nature, respect for personal integrity, production for a social purpose and not merely for the sake of production. These are all ideas that Mounier and Maritain had already expressed, beyond the great tradition of socialist thought.

Olivetti had one trauma in his life. He was a successful industrialist, well-read and an antifascist. In 1944, he had to emigrate from Italy for political reasons, thus sharing the fate of the Jewish people. He went to Switzerland, abandoning his company, which was the thing he held most dear, as is reflected in a very moving letter that mentioned Filippo Burzio, the worker who accompanied him and his father to America and with whom he analysed *Scientific Management*. Olivetti was already a big company, but Adriano Olivetti knew all his workers personally. By emigrating to Switzerland, he lost contact with his employees and witnessed the barbarism of fascism and Nazism: an additional trauma (still a wound that cannot be exorcised demagogically) was the extermination of the Jewish people. During this exile, he wrote an important book, which was to guide him throughout all his subsequent work (I have discussed some of this in an essay). It described everything he was attempting to do in Canavese from a practical, empirical viewpoint. In practice, it is easy to identify his messianic inspiration, which he implemented with striking errors (he was by no means perfect): Olivetti was particularly wrong in his choice of men—a mistake that utopians almost always make—putting himself into the hands of evildoers who then took advantage of his ideas.

He then wrote his book *L'ordine politico delle comunità*. The first edition was published by a typesetter in Switzerland in 1945 for the printing presses of Nuove Edizioni Ivrea. In Rome, a second print run was produced for Edizioni di Comunità in 1946. The subtitle of the last edition was "Of the state according to the laws of the spirit" and a very significant phrase was added as an epigraph to both editions: "Serving peace and Christian civilisation with the same will, the same intensity and the same audacity that were used for the purposes of oppression, destruction and terror". These words are important because they were written by a man who saw only catastrophe around him as he prepared his book: Hitler's armies were rampant; Mussolini still seemed invincible and had formidable propaganda tools to win over minds. Olivetti nevertheless believed that there was a possibility of serving peace and Christian civilisation. When he referred to Christian civilisation, he probably echoed T. S. Eliot, the great poet, who wrote a very important book, on principles of personal fulfilment that Olivetti published for the Comunità presses: *Christianity and Culture*. What did Olivetti write in his work? He attempted to explain how we can keep together the will to achieve freedom: "Freedom lives between the unjudged of the Gospel and the love of truth". He spoke of an economic third way beginning from the enterprise and going right up to the State organisation. What is the third way? Between state socialism, which Olivetti saw had already failed in the Soviet Union (through his contact with Trotskyist circles; the left-wing socialist circles that judged it so harshly), and full-blown economic liberalism, that is an uncontrolled market. "This plan—wrote Olivetti—is an attempt to fully describe a third way that meets multiple material and moral needs that have so far not been satisfied. This reform plan is underpinned by the concept of a new society that will be essentially socialist in orientation but must never ignore the two pillars of the society that preceded it: political democracy and individual freedom".

What is the essence of this book's contents? Neither the state alone nor the individual alone can respond to the great problems of the industrialised world that rose from the ruins of war and subsequently became established. The only way to respond to these immense problems is to reconstitute the unity of humankind between actions, thought and spirituality. And the only way to do this is again to allow humankind to live in what Olivetti refers to as a "concrete community". What is a concrete community? Olivetti bases his thought on a simple fact: there is a gulf between mankind and the State. An intermediate political organ must be created, that is the immediate community in which human beings live. As such, it is defined by the economic relations unfolding in the local fabric and the fiduciary, cultural and social relations unfolding in the men and women who manage that economy. The community must therefore have a human dimension: it must not be too small to prompt feelings of selfishness and competitiveness, or too large to reintroduce a relationship of alienation. The community must be medium-sized and relate to the organisational possibilities of local bodies. Olivetti thought basically of municipalities and groups of municipalities that must act as a pivot point, as bottom-up tools for self-regulating economic bodies acting in the community. The State must be both federalist and collectivist: the superiority of the community "lies in the great efficiency that comes from the specialisation intrinsic in the local skills of each community and the great ease with which citizens can get in touch with its bodies and control them".

A community must therefore be one cell of a new federal state. It is not federal as opposed to regional, but because it is made up of all communities, which are economic districts. Olivetti went on (thus making what I believed to be his serious mistake) to develop this idea, which had the potential to leaven all political forces, into his own political movement. Because he was effectively too cultured to create a political force through economic power, he used only intellectual power and therefore failed to achieve his goals. While organising this political movement, he even succeeded in promoting a community (of workers and managers) at the Fiat Mirafiori in Turin, because he thought that a great enterprise should be managed like a community. However, the fundamental idea of Olivetti's reform was that of a new democracy. What was this idea? We will leave aside the institutional architecture described in the work and look at the substance. Parliamentary democracies had failed and had not succeeded in halting fascism or Nazism. This had happened for two different reasons: because democratic political forces were not organised on a personalistic basis and because they did not make men and women, that is people, the centre of their activities. In other words, they did not base politics on the cultural elevation and emancipation of individual people. And they had not understood the relationship that the industrial nations were reshaping between the mechanism of competence and that of democracy. The response to the authoritarian systems of the 1930s was to limit democracy and Olivetti decided not to follow that route.

The fundamental principle, for him, had to be universal suffrage. It had to remain the democracy of the majority but avoid the dictatorship of the majority. Action had to be taken not on political demand but on political supply. In other words, the political class had to be selected based on their skills. In the life of the community, of democratic organisations, democracy had to be a kind of guided democracy (based on the Swiss model) in order to create a community on a human scale. The State had to be organised in such a way that only competent people were candidates for election to the highest state bodies. Olivetti believed that this could happen by means of a complex institutional architecture based on the main functions that the State should fulfil, from intervention in the economy to town planning. How could this purpose be achieved? By creating what he called the fundamental political institute. The state had to train the potential political class by creating an institution where individuals from every caste and class could enrol in and follow training courses over the years in order to create a kind of *pépinière*, or nursery for the political establishment. Pupils would have to train, take exams, be selected and be vastly superior to the possible electorate. This idea was therefore based on restricting the dictatorship of the majority, not at its base but at the top. Only competent people could therefore gain access to the highest echelons of state, but they should not be selected by civil society: Olivetti never spoke denigratingly about bare-headed child-like plebeians living in society—monsters roaming the contemporary forests. He believed that people must be educated directly through freedom and democracy and that a mechanism must be established that was capable of training the future political class. Some societies did it instinctively. For example, in France members of the political establishment are almost exclusively trained by the École Nationale d'Administration or by the École Nationale Polytechnique. This is not imposed by any law, it is the custom.

It could be said that the civilisation of a society is proportional to the institutionalisation of the training given to its political classes. Political classes should not be ruled by plebs but trained in special establishments. Olivetti's message was that the higher the level of institutionalisation in politics, the higher the level of civilisation. The more training is available for a broad and individualised ruling class, the more a society has evolved. But this cannot happen spontaneously. In his book, Olivetti analysed the most extreme institutional practice through the eyes of an entrepreneur and industrialist. The degree of civilisation is inversely proportional to the extent to which the training of the political classes is interested in economic power, mass media control, demagoguery and physiognomic traits (because people also vote on the basis of these aspects). Olivetti went so far as to say that this background should be regulated by State law. This is the reason his book is entitled *L'ordine politico delle comunità*, (The Political Order of Communities), that is an order that establishes intermediate societies between people and the State, who are able to select the ruling political class through the principle of competition: "A federal state of communities considers it a fundamental need to identify, train and organise a political élite fit to contribute to the creation of the new society and do so without any hint of privilege and exclusivity. This élite will be made up of a category of men and women who deeply feel their political vocation, in its true meaning of being a social mission. They will dedicate their lives to this exclusively". Olivetti is talking about professionalism. Who should select these impersonally selected élites (based on merit)? Olivetti wrote: "An individual is supported by material elements and is individualised and limited by that material. He or she therefore moves according to the outcome of a simple collision of forces, in a plane where spiritual laws cannot exert their invisible influence. If the world wishes to avoid new catastrophes and aim for higher goals, we must create a society where people are directly able to express their own humanity and spirituality [i.e. change from an individual to a person]".

How can this come about? Although Olivetti continued to be a man of the enlightenment, he was also a hands-on person in the style of Simone Weil. He maintained that the only way forward was to build social relationships in which individuals emancipate themselves and become people. According to him, social relations are guaranteed by a small-scale democracy, by self-organisation and above all by education and culture. Olivetti spent a huge proportion of his assets on a library and reduced the working hours of his workers so that they could take voluntary training courses. These were not strictly vocational and dealt with Roman history, the history of ancient Greece, cinema, philosophy and so on. Nowadays, 80% of the Ivrea public library is made up of the Olivetti library, even though Carlo De Benedetti ordered its voluntary destruction as soon as he took possession of the company to demonstrate his contempt for Adriano. Adriano was a practical and enlightened person because he believed there must always be an élite to drive the mechanism whereby individuals are changed into people. There had to be an original leadership group to educate the masses, primarily through schools. Olivetti did what Gianfranco Dioguardi is doing today. Dioguardi is the only enlightened entrepreneur to follow in Olivetti's footsteps. He donated Italian Liras (ITL) 300 million to a school in southernmost Italy, thus providing them with resources to achieve results despite their disadvantages. Albert Meinster (one of the theorists of cooperation who worked in Canavese and then set up cooperatives in southern Italy) described Olivetti as the embodiment of action to create an independent force for development, the first stage of which had to come about through help from above. He believed that an élite had to be present in order to encourage a groundswell from below. However, the process of changing from an individual to a person would not come about spontaneously. This huge responsibility had to be shouldered by private and public schools: it is the responsibility of any establishment educating young people. They also had to be trained in *Bildung*, as the Germans put it, that is a spiritual education: they had to be imbued with a civic sense as well as simply fed with information. Wanting this task to be entrusted to the well-meaning actions of an enlightened élite is perhaps a weakness of Olivetti's concept.

Olivetti also established part of the cooperative movement in the Canavese, where his position enabled him to do so, and later in southern

Italy (because he led great works to raise the morale of southern Italians, e.g. by helping to reclaim the "Sassi" of Matera). The difficulties he encountered were particularly related to his forward-thinking ideas about a third way. Nowadays we can see the splitting of the left between the Catholic and Communist worlds for the disaster it was. Despite their very different philosophical and supra-philosophical constructs, these two worlds stemmed from the same inspiration, that is to combine solidarity with efficiency and humanity: as Mounier said, they were based on the idea of the person. Both these great movements made enormous mistakes because they were bound and enslaved by power politics. We need only think of the disastrous consequences for the left-wing of joining the Soviet movement. Nowadays we can acknowledge that it failed because of the drive to identify with statism. Meanwhile, Catholicism made the mistake of identifying with the anti-Communist role of the Roman Catholic Church. Olivetti was much more far-sighted. This was his intellectual strength but also his weakness and the reason why he remains so fascinating. Both these movements achieved significant things, despite their mistakes. The cooperative movement came from the left and centre (not from the right). I believe that historians and economists can agree that the net balance of this movement was positive.

Olivetti wished to go beyond cooperation in order to establish a bottom-up socialisation of the economy based on his idea of a socialist federal state. Volkswagen, for example, represents a partial implementation of Olivetti's ideas. Most of the shares in this successful and competitive company are held by the *Land*, the German regional authority. It is owned not by a private owner but by a foundation. The company history included forced expropriation from the owning family, who were allied with the Nazis, and the company's subsequent socialisation by the Americans. It is a kind of municipal economy and Olivetti had in mind just such a venture, mid-way between cooperation and socialisation.

The Japanese idea of enterprise, on the other hand, is very far removed from Olivetti's ideas of community, particularly when considered in the light of Morishima's historical reflections on Japan's Shinto and Confucian cultural background. Today's Japanese enterprise community did not come about until the 1950s, when the Japanese trade union movement was physically mown down with machine guns in front of the factories (as happened in the US in the 1920s). What could the Japanese industry offer workers who had been left without a trade union? It could ensure jobs for life. The idea we have of the Japanese industry (a great model of efficiency) in Italy is largely the result of Japanese propaganda, promoted by Milan's Bocconi University. There certainly *is* an idea of community in Japan but of a very specific type. A Japanese psychoanalyst, Takeo Dai, wrote a very important book on Japanese culture, explaining that the principle of harmony lies at the basis of Japanese life. For example, Japanese mothers sleep with their children until they are seven to eight years old because in the Shinto culture the most destructive action is life, not death, which marks a reunion with one's being. This idea of community does not include the concept of I (there is no word in Japan with the etymological meaning of "I"). The Japanese idea of community implies the absence of the person: the person is annihilated by the collective. This idea is antithetical to an idea of community as emancipation of the person. Is Olivetti's idea of community realistic in an age of economic globalisation? He inhabited a world where the market was not yet global, and an idea had to be extended to continental level in order to be effective, otherwise social dumping would ensue. Olivetti nevertheless came up with a quintessentially modern idea: the value of the person.

If it is Europe's destiny today to aim at a form of industry with high intangible capital (in other words, technology and everything involved in the incorporation of science into the production process), know-how is fundamental to business. In anthropological terms, we have moved from a world of feet and farming through hands and industry on to a post-industrial world where the mind is central. Personal morality is now crucial because complex cognitive processes cannot be achieved through specialisation alone. Flexibility is important, but people must have broad training. This is why I believe that Olivetti's community-based personalism has a future: it focuses on the value of the person.

We could do worse than dust off the old Einaudi edition of Marx's economic and philosophical manuscripts, curated by Luigi Firpo. These contain the author's attempt, in the wake of Hegel and Feuerbach, to envisage men and women as the fulfilment of their species and genus, that is by being alive, but (as a good young Hegelian) also of their absolute spirit, thus incorporating the idea of reason and freedom. Men and women can only be fulfilled if the absolute spirit is present. The great driver of the absolute spirit was the bond between intellectuals and the people, to put it in Gramscian terms. Intellectuals were at various times the monks of the Dark Ages, followers of Boethius, nineteenth-century priests, socialist preachers, communists, priests who went among lepers to evangelise—anyone who sought the truth and tried to turn it into common sense: this was the link between intellectuals and people. The problem today is that this link is no longer present.

The current crisis, in Hegelian terms, can be attributed to concealment.

Index[1]

[1] Note: Page numbers followed by 'n' refer to notes.

G. Sapelli, *Beyond Capitalism*, https://doi.org/10.1007/978-3-030-20769-4

The manufacturer's authorised representative in the EU is Springer Nature Customer Service Centre GmbH, Europaplatz 3, 69115 Heidelberg, Germany. If you have any concerns regarding our products, please contact ProductSafety@springernature.com

Printed and bound by CPI Group (UK) Ltd, Croydon, CR0 4YY
25/09/2026
02222890-0002